A Sparrow's Tale

The story of Lavinia Abrol
one of God's much loved Sparrows

GLORIA KEARNEY
& LAVINIA ABROL

AMBASSADOR INTERNATIONAL
Greenville, South Carolina • Belfast, Northern Ireland

A SPARROW'S TALE

ISBN 978-1-84030-217-2

Ambassador Publications
a division of
Ambassador Productions Ltd.
Providence House
Ardenlee Street,
Belfast,
BT6 8QJ
Northern Ireland
www.ambassador-productions.com

Emerald House
427 Wade Hampton Blvd.
Greenville
SC 29609, USA
www.emeraldhouse.com

CONTENTS ❧

Introduction   5

Part One ❧
SING IN THE SHADOW

	Foreword	11
1	Lucy	13
2	I Baptise Thee	17
3	A New Name	20
4	Uncle Billy's	24
5	A Room Of My Own	28
6	Footsteps On The Stairs	31
7	An Angel Smiled	34
8	Cat In A Suitcase	38
9	Flying On Broken Wings	43
10	Appointments With God	46
11	A Little Bit Further	50
12	Romance And Revival	53
13	Stones, Bombs And Umbrellas	57
14	The God Of Miracles	61
15	Wedding Plans	65
16	Catreen	69
17	On The Road	76
18	If You Will Give Me A Son	84
19	Women Talking	90
20	Surrender	97
21	Please Don't Do This To Me	103
22	Country Living	108

23 Open House 114

24 Old Sins Cast Long Shadows 122

25 Behind The Fence 130

26 Passing It On ... 136

27 Touching Lives 143

28 Homesick For Heaven 147

29 The Valley Of The Shadow 155

30 We've Found The Child 165

31 Full Circle 173

32 Glimpses Of Hope 179

Part Two ❧
STILL SINGING

33 Robin's Dream 189

34 Canadian Adventure 195

35 Jesus Saviour Pilot Me 201

36 Paul Opens The Door 205

37 American Dream 211

38 On The Road Second Time Around 217

39 Terrible Paws 222

40 Loved With Everlasting Love 227

41 Restoration 233

42 More Than Enough 237

43 Alternative Lifestyle 243

44 Contentment 247

45 Monkey On A Stick 251

46 Answered Prayer 256

47 Autumn 260

Epilogue - Leaves in Autumn 265

INTRODUCTION ❦

Ten years ago my biography "Sing in the Shadow" was written by Gloria Kearney. Thousands of people read that book. After ten years we decided that the time had come to stop having it reprinted. However people still asked for it and when I went out to speak in churches, were disappointed when they could not get the book anymore. There were those who had not read it and there were others who had given their copies away and wanted to replace them. The question we asked was, "What now?"

This is the result, a revised and updated edition of "Sing in the Shadow". The original story is still here with accompanying photographs. There is also much more as it brings the story up to date and also has chapters on lessons learnt along the way. This is "A Sparrow's Tale".

The book's title comes from Matthew ch10 v29.

"Are not two sparrows sold for a penny? Yet not one of them will fall to the ground apart from the will of your Father........ so do not be afraid, you are worth more than many sparrows."

This is one of my favourite scriptures. I have always felt like His wee sparrow. I have known His protection, I have known His care and I have known His love. There have been times when like a wounded bird, I felt Him pick me up off the ground and hold me close to His heart. Holding me gently He tended my wounds, repaired my bruised body and let me rest. As I rested in His care and stayed close to His heartbeat, I would hear His voice of love encouraging me.

"Fly little one," He would say.

Renewed with His strength and with hope in my heart, once again I would find my wings.

While writing this introduction, one of my dear friends, Freda, sent me a piece of writing by Selwyn Hughes about sparrows. In it he made the comment that while swallows dart off to the sun, sparrows stay and brave the stormy blast. I had never thought of that before. They are resilient little birds that stay with us here in Britain all year round. In the cold of winter they struggle to keep warm and must often find it hard to survive. They too know about struggle.

Ira Stamphill penned it well in his song "I don't know about tomorrow." The second verse says,

> *"I don't know about tomorrow,*
> *It may bring me poverty,*
> *But the one who feeds the sparrow*
> *Is the one who stands by me.*
> *And the path that be my portion,*
> *May be through the flame or flood.*
> *Still His presence goes before me,*
> *And I'm covered with His blood."*

In the gospels when Luke tells the story of God's care for the sparrows, he writes it a different way. Matthew tells us that 2 birds are sold for a penny. Luke tells us that 5 birds are sold for two pennies. In other words if you spent 2 pennies, a fifth sparrow was thrown in free. This was probably a bird that was so small it could not have been sold. Commercially it did not have a price tag, it was something so useless that it was given away. Yet I believe it was mentioned in this story because in God's eyes it had value. It is mentioned because in God's economy, it had significance. In God's economy, nothing is useless and nothing is wasted.

This is God's nature. This is unconditional love - there is no such thing as nuisance value with Him. There is no-one beyond God's love. He reaches down through the shame and despair, the loneliness and pain, the regrets and the disillusionment, He picks up broken and wounded men and women and He puts value on them. A Sparrow's Tale has been written to give hope and courage to those who find their names written on that Fifth Sparrow. Perhaps you can identify with the past few paragraphs. You may wonder if you will ever be able to rise again. How will you ever make it through? You are too damaged, the fall was too great. Will you ever be free from the pain?

I too have felt those things throughout my life. Some you will read about in this book but not all. My prayer is that you will know God's healing grace in your life. The Bible says that He is the Redeemer of all things. He redeems our souls and He redeems our past. I see my name written on that Fifth Sparrow, but I also see it engraved on His hands. He is my greatest joy, He is my heart's song. He is my peace.

Come, let me tell you a tale of a much loved sparrow.

Lavinia

Part One ❧

 SING IN THE SHADOW

THANKS ❧

Thank you to …

Lavinia for agreeing to let me write her story and supplying tea and tissues while we worked together on it …

Robert, Tamara, Marcus and Lysander who have so cheerfully put up with an untidy house and scrappy meals so that Mum could "write" …

Pat, the third member of our prayer triplet, who painstakingly typed the manuscript and encouraged us by her prayers …

Michael, who so willingly agreed to provide the illustrations and who so graciously allowed them to be replaced by photographs in this new edition…

All those who allowed a little of their own stories to be told within Lavinia's.

I couldn't have done it without you.

Gloria

FOREWORD ❧

There are times when I choked back the tears and times when I rocked with laughter as I read this book ... often on the same page! It's that kind of book. You cannot read it and remain detached; the warmth and detail draw you in. Reflective, funny, sad, challenging, controversial and more, but never boring. There are some extraordinary twists and turns in Lavinia's story but even ordinary people and ordinary events assume a fascination because of her wonderful capacity to observe, recall and relate little gems of detail. Detail so often missed by the rest of us, yet full of colour and drama. I find myself looking and listening more carefully since I read this book.

Lavinia sees the strengths and weaknesses of Northern Ireland from a rare perspective of a woman who was raised on one side of the "peace line", only to discover that she has much from the other side in her blood. Secretly she treasures the mixture. There is hope in that for us all.

Lavinia has been shaped by our divided society but she has stubbornly refused to be distorted by it. She has found in Gloria Kearney a writer who has managed to allow very little of herself to creep in between the reader and the story.

Hadden Wilson
Former Pastor, Ballynahinch Baptist Church

Chapter 1 🐦
LUCY

28th June 1951.

"You have a lovely baby girl. Would you like to hold her?"

Lucy didn't reply but simply turned her face to the wall and the nurse was somewhat taken aback to see a tear trickle slowly down her cheek. This was not the usual response to the birth of a child and she was unsure how to react.

I'll leave the baby in the cot beside you. Maybe you'll feel better later on," she said as she turned to leave the ward.

Lucy kept her head firmly turned away from the baby as she fought to gain control. Her angry thoughts jostled inside her head ...

"Feel better later on? - I'll never feel better, never again! Would I like to hold her? - I'm afraid to hold her! As long as I don't hold her, I won't love her. A lovely baby girl? - Is she lovely? I'm afraid to look - If she's lovely, I won't be able to say goodbye to her." The baby gave a little cry and Lucy's resistance broke down. She sat up in the bed and turned to look at the tiny baby lying there. She was beautiful and the love that

Lucy feared might rise in her heart, welled up and would not be quenched. She stroked the little hand and whispered, "Oh, what a mess, what an awful mess. How can I give you up?"

As Lucy sat on the edge of her bed in the Maternity Ward of what later became the Jubilee Hospital, watching her baby daughter through tear-filled eyes, the memories of the past year flooded back. The previous summer had been a carefree one. She had a handsome boyfriend, an air-force man called James and the days had been filled with laughter. The fact that he was a Catholic and she was a Protestant didn't matter at all to them.

The realisation that Lucy was pregnant brought an abrupt end to the carefree days. James, or Seamus as his family called him, was keen to marry her and at first it seemed a good idea. She agreed to receive instruction in the Catholic church but her mother and brother were fiercely opposed to her becoming a Catholic.

"If you do," they told her, "you will never again put your foot over the door of this house." In the end, the pressure from her family was too great and she could not go through with the marriage and the change of religion.

She ran her hand gently over the baby's soft fine hair and a wave of self-pity swept over her. How had it come to this? Thirty-one years old, unmarried, with a new baby and now faced with the most awful dilemma of all. Her face distorted in pain as she remembered her brother's reaction to the news, that Lucy wanted to bring up the child on her own at home.

"I'll not have it. You needn't think you're bringing another brat into my house!"

Although Lucy's mother was still alive, the house in which they lived belonged to Billy and his word was law. She knew better than to go against his wishes as he had a fierce temper that frequently erupted into violence.

"It's all so unfair," Lucy thought. "Nellie was allowed to keep her baby."

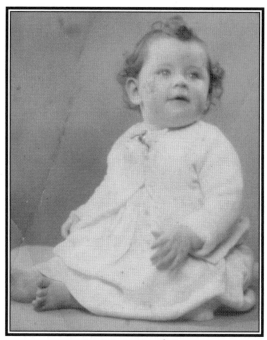

Lavinia at 10 months.

The irony of the fact that she had helped to rear her sister's illegitimate child for most of the past seven years since Nellie had left to get married, but would not now be allowed to rear her own, hit Lucy afresh and she lay across the bed weeping as though her heart would break.

Her only consolation was that James' mother had agreed to take the child and she knew that they would love her and give her a new home. It wasn't what her heart longed for but it was a solution to her immediate dilemma. Just a few days later, Lucy stood at the ward door, face pale and her eyes full of pain as James' mother walked down the corridor with her tiny baby daughter. Though she could hardly see through her tears, she watched until the swing doors at the far end of the corridor clicked shut.

Lucy had no way of knowing but Someone else watched the sad little scene that day. God had a plan for the child in Granny Bingham's arms - a plan more wonderful than the best that Lucy could have wished for her little daughter.

Chapter 2 ❧

I BAPTISE THEE

Granny Bingham laid the baby in the big black pram in the hall. She was a little plump lady, well known in the local community for her organisational skills and her charitable deeds. People from all around looked to her for advice and support. Her neighbours' religion made little difference to her - she was just as likely to encourage the Protestant neighbour a few doors away to send her children to Sunday School as she was to encourage her own to go to Chapel. Needy people were helped or even taken in to live in her own home.

She enjoyed life and her hearty laugh was often heard in the house, particularly when everyone gathered in for one of her famous lemonade parties. Her own family was almost reared - the youngest, Margaret Mary was twelve and some of the older ones had already left home. They had grown up in an atmosphere of firm discipline and love and music. Willie John and Paddy could play the piano by ear. Margaret Mary had been given lessons and one of their favourite ways to spend an evening was to have a singsong in the parlour.

"Well," thought Granny Bingham, looking down into the pram, "there's nothing else for it. If Lucy can't keep you, we'll give you a home."

She had suspected that this might happen, knowing how Lucy's brother felt about Catholics, and had made plans just in case. Seamus might have behaved badly and his mother had left in him no doubt about how deeply ashamed she was of his foolishness but none of it was the child's fault and Maria Bingham was not prepared to let the baby suffer as a result.

Her own children were told nothing of her plans. Margaret Mary was encouraged to go for a long holiday at her cousin's house in England, possibly to save her being upset if it didn't work out. When, a few days later, Eileen, her eldest married daughter came to visit, she was surprised to see a pram in the hallway.

"Whose is the baby?" she enquired.

"It's the one I'm adopting," was the reply.

Eileen looked at her mother in astonishment.

"Are you mad in the head?" she asked.

Granny Bingham shook her head.

"Sure it's Seamus' wee daughter, what else could I do?"

Over a cup of tea, the two women discussed the new arrival and Granny Bingham confided in her daughter that she didn't think they would be able to keep her for long.

"Someone has sent word that Lucy is coming to take her back ... to tell you the truth, Eileen, I'm worried about it."

"Why are you worried, Ma, sure the child would be better off with its mother."

"It's not that," Granny Bingham replied, "I'm not sure if they'll have her baptised. I don't believe they're a God fearing family, they mightn't bother. I'll not be happy if she's not baptised and I don't know what to do."

"Well," said Eileen, "there is a remedy. We'll baptise her ourselves."

It was no sooner said than done. Eileen fetched a jug of water from the kitchen and took the tiny baby, who had been given the names Mary Kathleen, in her arms. Watched by Grandfather Bingham, Granny Bingham and Thomas, Eileen sprinkled some water on the baby's head and pronounced the words,

"I baptise thee in the name of the Father and of the Son and of the Holy Spirit."

A day or two later, it was Granny Bingham's turn to have tears in her eyes as she watched Mary Kathleen being carried down her front path in Lucy's arms. She had known the pain of parting before but never the uncertainty of this relinquishment. She felt that she was handing over her own son's daughter to an unknown future in which she would have little part and the pain was like a knife in her heart.

Some weeks later, Margaret Mary heard that her mother had thought of adopting a baby. She didn't believe the story and went to Granny Bingham to find out the truth. Her mother told her what had happened and explained that she couldn't keep the baby because its mother wanted her back. She finished her story by giving Margaret a charge that the twelve year old girl took very seriously and would remember for the rest of her life.

"I want you to pray for Mary Kathleen," she said

So from that time on, a young Belfast Catholic girl prayed earnestly for a little Protestant baby. One of her prayers was that God would love her … and He did!

Chapter 3 ❧

A New Name

"Where have Aunt Lucy and Aunt Jessie gone?" Isobel asked her Granny. "I saw them going off in Nurse Green's car a wee while ago."

A ride in the car belonging to the district nurse, who lived next door, usually meant that something important was happening and Isobel, Nellie's daughter, was determined to find out what it was.

Granny Johnston took a moment or two to reply but eventually told her,

"They've gone to get your Aunt Lucy's baby."

"Maybe now Aunt Lucy will stop crying," thought Isobel.

The past week had been awful. Aunt Lucy had gone into hospital to have her baby but had come home without her. Since then she had spent every day in tears and at night Isobel had heard her sobbing in her bedroom. The whole household had been upset by it and eventually Billy had snarled at Lucy the previous night to go and get the brat.

"I might as well listen to it snivelling as you. So shut yer trap and do what you have to do," he had yelled.

Although she didn't say much, Isobel was secretly quite pleased at the thought of a baby in the house. As the only child in a household of adults, she was often lonely and rather liked the idea of feeding and dressing her little cousin. She even wondered if a baby might make everyone a bit happier. Her grandmother, though kind enough to her, was strict, her Uncle Billy always seemed to be cross and ill-tempered, her Aunt Lucy flared up at the slightest provocation and Isobel still felt keenly the sense of rejection she had known on the day seven years before when her mother had driven off to a new life, leaving her seven year old daughter behind. A little happiness was long overdue.

So Mary Kathleen came home. Nurse Green bought a beautiful big pram and a pram set and Isobel was allowed to wheel the new baby up and down the street in the warm sunshine of the long July days.

She was the one sent to answer the door when James' younger brother would call with an envelope for Lucy. Isobel couldn't understand why James no longer came but she didn't like to ask too many questions and no one wanted to talk about it. She was happy enough to be sent to the door for the young man was good-looking and pleasant but her Granny was afraid of history repeating itself and Isobel was given instructions just to take the envelope and not talk to him.

After just a week or two, it became apparent that all was not well with the new baby. She was irritable and cried a lot and at first Lucy put it down to the heat but when Mary Kathleen was sick three or four times in a row, she realised that it was more serious. The doctor who was consulted had the baby admitted to Purdysburn Hospital where gastritis was diagnosed, a serious illness in such a young baby.

When Lucy was brought in to see her little one, she had to dress in a gown and mask before being allowed into the isolation ward where Mary Kathleen lay in a tiny cot. She looked so small and helpless, so pale and lifeless. Lucy tried to gain encouragement from the nurses and doctors but they were very reluctant to offer much hope. Some babies had already died of this illness.

Despite the fact that the Purdysburn Hospital was situated quite a few miles out from Belfast, Lucy managed to visit most days but it was obvious that Mary Kathleen was not making much progress. So when a policeman arrived at the house one day with a telegram in his hand, Lucy imagined the worst. When she finally plucked up courage to open the telegram she read the words, "Come to hospital immediately, Mary much worse."

Every inch of the journey to Purdysburn felt like a mile and with each step along the corridor her feet felt more leaden. The ward sister spoke to her before letting her go into the ward and warned her that Mary's condition was causing great concern. In fact they were afraid that she might not last the night.

Lucy put on her gown and mask and slowly made her way to the little cot. For the second time in her baby's short life, Lucy wept at the thought of saying goodbye to her.

"I thought everything would be wonderful when I finally got you home," she cried. "I've had so little time with you - you can't die on me now."

As Lucy paced up and down beside the cot, wishing there was something she could do, Nurse Greer, who had gone to the hospital with her, tried to comfort her. One of the nurses suggested that it might be a good idea to have the baby christened.

"You know," she said gently, "she might not make it through the night."

Although Lucy wasn't a religious person, she still felt it was important to have her baby christened, if only for death and agreed for the hospital chaplain to come. At least this was something she could do for her little daughter. Nurse Greer had become rather fond of her neighbour's baby and made a rather special request.

"Lucy - she'll not be long with us, will you give her my name?"

Lucy was happy to grant the request for Nurse Greer had been very good to her, giving her as much support as she could in her difficult circumstances. So the baby, who had been

Lavinia aged two.

baptised into the Catholic Church as Mary Kathleen, was baptised again into the Protestant church as Lavinia Mary Kathleen.

Now content that she had done right by her child, Lucy spent an anxious night listening to her laboured breathing and distressed crying. But Lavinia was a fighter and a survivor and when morning came she was still alive and had even shown a slight improvement. She would spend a long time in hospital but the crisis had passed and she would get better.

In the same ward, and as a result of the same illness, another baby girl fought for her life too. The two mothers exchanged names and shared their worries and fears about their babies. They had absolutely no idea that the lives of Lavinia Johnston and Maisie Hall would be so closely interwoven in the years ahead but God above knew the plan He had made and sent His angel to walk the ward, in His mercy sparing their lives from death, in order to bring His purposes for them to fruition.

Chapter 4 ❧

UNCLE BILLY'S

Lavinia continued to make good progress and returned to live at Uncle Billy's house on the Shore Road. Isobel was delighted that her little cousin had survived and as the baby grew and began to walk and talk, Isobel and she became very close, more like sisters than cousins. Lavinia wasn't very old when it became obvious that she had a great sense of fun. She was full of mischief and particularly liked hiding things around the house. Unfortunately she discovered that one of the best hiding places was down the toilet - things really disappeared when she put them there!

She loved throwing things and would realise in later life that this habit had been inherited from her mother. Her favourite way to greet Isobel was to throw something at her.

Her mischievous ways and her wilful nature often got her into trouble. She wasn't very old when she found out how Lucy dealt with trouble - she kept a bamboo cane. Sometimes Lucy flared up so quickly that she didn't have the patience to find the cane and simply lashed out with her fist. Both girls felt the weight of Lucy's fist on their nose on many occasions.

At a very early stage, Lavinia realised with the sharp intuition of a child, that Uncle Billy didn't want to have anything to do with her. He barely spoke to her mother, just snarled at her when absolutely necessary and fiercely resented having this baby in the house. Even the child's near death hadn't softened him and both Lavinia and Isobel avoided him when they could and did their best to keep in his good books when they couldn't.

When Granny Bingham and Aunt Margaret Mary brought a present for Lavinia's second birthday, it was Uncle Billy who insisted that there was to be no more contact with the Catholic side of the family. Lucy had to tell them as they left that day, that it would be better if they didn't visit again. Uncle Billy paid the rent and so he had to be obeyed.

Lavinia had a warmer relationship with Granny Johnston. She always seemed to sit in the same chair and always had sweets for the girls in the pocket of the big apron she wore. When Lavinia started Lowood Primary School, she used to sit beside her grandmother and tell her about all her new experiences. School was an exciting place which she thoroughly enjoyed. She loved having friends of her own age, she loved skipping in the playground at break times, she loved the very smell of school, a strange mixture of chalk and books and disinfectant.

She was encouraged to sing in school and played the part of an angel in her first Nativity play. When Lucy realised that her little girl enjoyed singing, she began to enter her for talent competitions in the Lido and the Troxy. Lavinia learnt songs like "Snowy Flakes are Falling" and Isobel and her new boyfriend, Albert, bought pretty dresses for her to wear. Being on stage held few fears for her, in fact she loved performing, and these early years were a wonderful preparation for a time to come when she would stand in pulpits and stages singing the praises of the One who would come to mean everything to her.

One afternoon during her first year in school, Lucy, who usually collected her at the gate, was late. Eventually one of the neighbours arrived to bring Lavinia home. She ran in to say hello to her granny, who was sitting as usual, in her chair with her feet up. Before she reached Granny, she realised her mother was crying, in hysterics, and Lavinia hesitated, wondering what was wrong. Nurse Greer, who was also in the room, rushed over and pushed both Lavinia and Lucy out of the door, closing it firmly behind them. Lucy shouted and cried and kicked the door in her desperation to get back inside. She kept calling out for her mother and Lavinia began to feel afraid. Whatever was the matter?

Lucy gave her no explanation but in a little while the door opened and Nurse Greer brought them back into the room, explaining as simply as possible to Lavinia that her Granny Johnston, who was still sitting in her chair, had just died.

"We'd better open the window and let her soul go out," she said.

Lavinia watched to see, but nothing happened and she was left wondering what the nurse had meant. Soon afterwards, she was sent to a neighbour's house to stay while the funeral arrangements were made. When Granny Johnston had been laid out in her coffin, Lavinia was brought to the house to see her. It was her first experience of death and it made her feel afraid, but despite her fear, one of the adults lifted her up to look at the body in the coffin. Her Granny looked strange - very still, very white - and Lavinia was glad when she was put down and could run out of the room.

After Granny Johnston's death, the atmosphere in the house changed and the tension between Billy and Lucy worsened. By the time Lavinia was seven, Isobel and Albert's romance had become serious and they married. Lucy found life at Uncle Billy's increasingly difficult and began to look for a way out for herself and her child. She chose a rather unconventional method - the personal column in the Belfast Telegraph. One of the advertisements caught her eye, she replied to it and began seeing a man called Davey Williams, who lived on the Shankill Road.

After a short courtship, Lucy agreed to marry him. Lavinia, who had enjoyed attending Isobel's wedding and presenting the bride with a horseshoe, was disappointed that she wasn't allowed to go to her mother's wedding. It was a quiet affair, held in a Registry Office and Lavinia was left at home with a friend. It brought many new things into the little girl's life - a new stepfather, a new name, a new home.

Chapter 5 ❧

A ROOM OF MY OWN

Lavinia had mixed feelings about the move to Shankill Road. Her biggest concern was how she would cope in a new school with new teachers, new classmates, new routines and new rules. She would have been even more apprehensive had she realised that this move would herald the beginning of a total of fourteen school moves in the next few years. On the other hand, she was looking forward to having her own bedroom. In Uncle Billy's house she shared, not just her Mum's bedroom, but her Mum's bed, and the prospect of having a room of her own was an attractive one.

The room itself, the back bedroom in the little two-up, two-down terraced house, was not much by today's standards. A single bed was the only piece of furniture, her clothes were hung on nails driven into the back of the door and her shoes were stored under the bed. Lavinia was a creative little girl and she soon added a most important piece of furniture - a bedside cabinet. The greengrocer was probably not greatly surprised by her request for an orange box but he might have been surprised if he had seen what she did with it. It was turned on its side so that the central division became a shelf and then lovingly covered in pink and white striped wallpaper. She put it in position beside her bed and placed in it some of her most prized possessions - her books.

Lucy could never understand her daughter's obsession with books and a visit to NPO to spend her pocket money inevitably resulted in the following conversation.

"What do you want to buy?"

"A book."

"Why do you always want to waste your money on a book? Why don't you buy sweets or toys?"

"I like books."

"Money's hard enough to come by without you throwing it away on books."

Lavinia usually got her way and soon the pink and white bedside cabinet was full of titles like 'What Katy Did', 'Polly of Primrose Hill' and 'Lavender at High School'. What Lavinia couldn't explain to her mother and may not even have understood herself was that the books were an escape into a wonderful fantasy world where she could be a princess in a castle, or go to boarding school or own a dog. They provided a window into a place where she would no longer be Lavinia from the Shankill. As time went on and her own life became increasingly difficult to handle, they became, not just an escape, but a lifeline.

A shoebox, also covered in wallpaper, became Lavinia's treasure box. In it she kept some writing paper made from scrap paper from her school books, rings from lucky bags, and any pretty sparkly things that she could find. Curled neatly into coils on the top were her hair ribbons. Lavinia loved her hair ribbons and Lucy enjoyed tying back her long black hair or plaiting it in two braids, securing it with the hair ribbons. The only thing that neither of them enjoyed was the Saturday night bath time ritual, so necessary for beautiful curls. After washing in the tin bath brought in from the back yard each Saturday night, Lavinia would sit in front of the fire while her mother put her hair into rags. To make the desired ringlets, the hair had to be tied tightly into the rags, a process usually accompanied by squeals of protest and sometimes even tears.

And so for a little while life for Lucy and Lavinia developed a satisfactory pattern. Davey went off to work each day, while Lavinia went to the school into which she had settled happily enough and Lucy cleaned and polished her new home, even scrubbing both the windowsills and a half moon around the door every day.

Chapter 6 🐦

FOOTSTEPS ON THE STAIRS

The voices in the kitchen downstairs reached a crescendo and Lavinia awoke with a start.

"What do you mean, woman - there's not enough money? It's my money and don't you forget it!"

A chair scraped on the floor as it was flung out of the way and a dish smashed against the wall as Lucy's temper also flared.

"I can't feed you on nothing," she yelled. "You come home stinkin' of drink with not a penny in your pocket and you expect me to have dinner on the table? Food doesn't grow on trees you know!"

Lavinia heard a thump and a scream from her mother and her stomach felt sick as she realised that her stepfather was beating Lucy once again. She held on tightly to the quilt and hoped it would soon be over.

The door of the kitchen opened and the noise got louder as Lucy threw herself after Davey, flinging a milk bottle in his direction for good measure. Lavinia heard the smash of glass as it broke in pieces on the stairs.

"There would be more money if it wasn't for that good-for-nothin' brat of yours. Where is she anyway?" roared Davey.

Lavinia sat up in bed and started to shake as she heard her mother yell after him - "You leave her out of this."

His heavy footsteps thumped on the stairs and with each thump Lavinia's heart beat faster. This was the sound she had come to dread. He reached the top of the stairs and as her door burst open, Lavinia leapt out of bed in a vain attempt to escape the blows.

"Come 'ere you. You're gonna get what you deserve."

With a mighty heave he tossed the bed aside and reached for the little girl who was cowering against the wall. Lucy launched herself at him again and managed to pull him off balance away from Lavinia but not before he grabbed her arm and flung her roughly against the bed. She lay whimpering in pain while Lucy, with the strength of desperation, hauled Davey out of the door and into their bedroom.

The fight continued until the early hours of the morning and Lavinia winced at the sound of every blow as she tried to sort out her bed again. She crawled into it shaking with fear and shivering with cold as the draught from yet another broken window whistled under her door. Curling up into a ball, she pulled the bedclothes tightly round her and lay, too upset to sleep, wondering if there were any homes where mothers and fathers lived without fighting and where children lived without the fear of being hurt every day.

Scenes from the past few months flashed through her mind. It hadn't taken long for them to realise that the move to Davey's house had proved to be a bit like jumping from the frying pan into the fire. Lavinia had a healthy respect for Uncle Billy's uncertain temper but it was mild compared with her stepfather's drunken rages. He lost much of his money on gambling and was drunk almost every night. Lucy and he were strong-willed individuals, neither of whom liked to lose an argument and the inevitable clash of wills over even the most insignificant issues would erupt in mighty battles that resulted in beatings, broken furniture and smashed windows.

Eventually it had got too much for Lucy and after a particularly vicious beating, Lucy and Lavinia had gathered up their few possessions and crept out of the house while Davey slept, to seek refuge at Uncle Billy's. Lavinia felt her bruises hurt as she turned over in the bed and wished with all her heart that they had stayed at Uncle Billy's. She knew, of course, why her mother had returned and she felt despair rise in her as she remembered the letters that had arrived and her uncle's agitation as he read the threats they contained.

"You'll have to go back." he told Lucy. "He's threatening to put the bully boys on me if you stay here."

Lucy was further persuaded by Davey's assurances that things would be different, that he would change. She had nowhere else to go and he was a good enough man when he was sober. Lavinia had cried for most of the journey back to the Shankill Road and now, as the sounds of the fighting subsided, she turned her face to the pillow and cried again. No one came to comfort her and she sobbed quietly till sleep brought welcome oblivion.

❦

Chapter 7 ❧

AN ANGEL SMILED

For Lavinia, life became a bewildering kaleidoscope that left her confused and insecure. Some moments were good - evenings when Davey took out his accordion and entertained them in the front room, days when they went on outings like any normal family. The trip to Donaghadee was a very good day - Davey treated them to a meal out and posed for a picture with his arm around his wife in affection rather than anger.

These were rare occurrences and many of the good moments took place outside the home. She was allowed to join the Girl Guides and Lucy reluctantly agreed for her to attend some children's meetings. Her reluctance may have had something to do with the name of the place where they were held - The Dump! Lavinia was drawn to these meetings by the warm feeling of peace she experienced there, a peace that was unknown at home. In that little room, the God who had a plan for her, began to reach down to that lonely, broken little girl and she, in her turn, began a search for something she didn't fully understand but that she felt would bring her the peace and security she lacked.

She was conscious of a similar feeling of peace in a church and once again was given somewhat reluctant permission to go to church and Sunday School at St Matthew's on the Woodvale Road. She understood nothing about the presence of God but just walking into a church had a powerful effect on her. She had a sense that here was something not of this world and she wondered if she might find what she needed in that place. The leaders at 'The Dump' had talked a lot about "becoming a Christian" so she asked the Minister one day if he knew how to become a Christian. He seemed somewhat unsure what to say to this little girl but quoted a very famous verse from the Bible.

"Lavinia, just believe on the Lord Jesus Christ and you will be saved."

No other explanation was offered but even so, it was enough to send Lavinia skipping home. She ran into the house to find her rope, skimmed up the lamp-post across the road, attached the rope to the top, clambered down again, settled herself on a cushion on the improvised swing, then gently swung round and round, all the while whispering to herself "I do believe in Jesus."

It wasn't a conversion experience but it was the beginning of a journey from darkness to light, a first step on the road to Jesus, the One who came to bring light to the world. As she swung around the lamp-post in childish delight, somewhere close by an angel smiled.

Other moments were dark and difficult and it seemed to Lavinia that anything good that came into her life was eventually snatched away. She loved to dance and begged to get going to dance lessons. Her mother managed to buy a pair of second-hand tap shoes and Lavinia threw herself into the lessons but by the time she outgrew the shoes, there was no money to buy new ones and the dancing had to stop.

Animals became another passion and on a few occasions she was given a kitten, only to have it cruelly drowned and left for her to find after one of Davey's drunken binges. As Davey became more and more unreasonable, he took some sort of perverse pleasure in thinking up mindless cruelties to inflict on his wife and stepdaughter. He would remove the fuses so that they would have to sit in the dark and throw water on the fire so that they would have no heat. Then, if he wanted a fire, he would think nothing of breaking up a piece of furniture to save buying coal.

Many of Lavinia's injuries were the result of her trying to stop the fighting or going to the aid of whoever needed most help. Lucy was just as quick to lash out as Davey and on one occasion went for him with a knife, managing to split his lip. Lavinia tried to go to his rescue but Lucy turned on her and punched her up the nose. The sight of the blood flowing from both of them stopped that fight more quickly than many others.

One evening when she was in her bedroom, she heard Lucy call out, "Lavinia, Lavinia, help me! He's got a knife!"

She rushed out to the landing to find Davey with a bread knife pointing at Lucy's chest. Without thinking of the consequences, Lavinia jumped in between them, grabbing the knife and pushing it away from her mother. Unfortunately she grabbed the blade and as the blood ran down to the floor, she realised that the top of her finger had almost been severed.

Lucy ran out of the house in panic, down to the police station and Lavinia ran to the sink to wash the blood away, then wrapped a towel around her hand in an attempt to hold it all together. Davey slumped down at the top of the stairs and started to cry. Since neither Lucy nor Davey was going to be much use to her, she went to a neighbour's house for help. She was brought to hospital and her finger was stitched back together again.

One of the most difficult aspects of this dark period in Lavinia's life was the uncertainty. She never knew whether to expect a smile or a slap, she never knew if there would be food on the table or if she would have to go hungry, she never knew when her mother would suddenly decide she couldn't face any more and she would be hurried away to stay at Uncle Billy's or in a rented room, or even in a police station. She never knew when a new day would mean a new school and as a result her education suffered a great deal. Some things she never learnt at all and other things she learnt over and over again. She often came home from school to find her mother packing for yet another house move, in the vain hope that a fresh start would mean a better life.

It was not to be, for there was a pub on every corner in the Shankill and after a few days it would be back to the old routine.

"You'd better go and find your father," Lucy would say. "It's time he was home, his dinner will be all dried up."

Lucy was often too ashamed of her battered appearance to go out, so Lavinia was sent to hunt for Davey.

"Do I have to go?"

Lavinia disliked this errand above all others.

"Could we not just leave him there? Could we not put the lights out and hide behind the chairs in the parlour like we did before? He'll think we're not in and just go to bed."

"No Lavinia, it's better if we get him home before he's too drunk. Go on, there's a good girl."

So Lavinia would set off, hating every moment. She hated the musty, boozy smell when she opened the pub doors, she hated the way all the men at the bar turned round to look at her, she hated the weight of the drunken man on her shoulders as she led him home, she hated having to stop to let him vomit in the gutter. The sense of shame she experienced as she led him along the streets would live with her forever.

Chapter 8 ❧

CAT IN A SUITCASE

"Lavinia!"

"Yes Mammy?"

Lavinia had just come in from school and was running through the kitchen to find Darkie, the cat, when Lucy stopped her.

"I've washed as many of your clothes as I can find and I don't want you to wear them till Saturday."

"What's happening on Saturday?"

"You know I've been telling you that we might be leaving here? Well we're really going - on Saturday."

Lavinia, who was now about eleven years old, had heard Lucy talk so often about leaving that she no longer paid too much attention to it but a new determination in her mother's voice made her look up with fresh hope.

"Do you really mean it, Mammy?"

"Can you keep a secret, Lavinia?" asked Lucy.

Lavinia nodded.

"I've got a new job as a housekeeper for someone, and I start on Monday."

"Where are we going this time?" asked Lavinia.

"Across the water to England," was the surprising reply.

Lavinia was torn between feelings of relief at getting away from Davey Williams and concern at all the implications of a move as drastic as this. She suddenly thought of Darkie, her beloved cat and she grabbed her Mum's arm in alarm.

"What about Darkie, I can't leave him behind!"

Lucy tried to argue that Darkie would survive but Lavinia would not be convinced.

"He'll be done away with! He's only lasted so long because I look out for him all the time. If he can't go, I'm not going!"

The argument went on for a day or two but Lavinia was adamant and eventually Lucy gave in. Darkie would go with them.

Their meagre possessions were carefully and secretly packed into one suitcase and newspapers were put into another for Darkie and off they set for Birmingham. The hole made in the top of the suitcase to provide air for Darkie was too big and the cat kept poking his head out to see what was going on. Lavinia kept pushing his head back down, talking to the cat to calm him and the journey by boat and train passed uneventfully enough.

Lucy's new employer met them at the train and brought them to his home. Lucy's heart sank when she saw it - to call it a filthy hole would be an understatement! Eight cats roamed at will all over the kitchen and the house hadn't been cleaned for months. She wasn't afraid of hard work, however, and spent the first week in her new home going from room to room, scrubbing and cleaning. Lavinia was concerned how Darkie would settle in with the other cats but they all seemed friendly enough and there appeared to be no problems.

And so over the next few weeks Lavinia started to relax. She made friends in the street, got accustomed to the Birmingham accent, discovered that for the first time in her life, she was ahead of the children in her class and revelled in the feeling of being clever. She found her mother's employer to be a pleasant, friendly man who liked to take her on his knee and

*Lavinia and Darkie, the cat who travelled
in a suitcase.*

chat to her and she no longer had to dread each evening and what it might bring.

For Lucy, it was a different experience and as Lavinia relaxed, she became more tense. She too found her employer friendly - too friendly. It became obvious as time went on that he wanted her to be more than a housekeeper and Lucy found it more and more difficult to fend off his unwelcome attentions. The first indication that Lavinia had that something was wrong was when her mother began putting a chair under the handle of the door at night. She sensed the tension in Lucy even though her mother wouldn't fully explain the reason for her fears.

As a result, an idea began to formulate in the young girl's mind, an idea that would mar her relationships with men for years to come - men were bad and were not to be trusted. It could of course have developed into a much worse situation but as Lavinia sat in innocent trust on that man's knee, the angel who watched, said, "Enough!" and a hedge of protection was placed about her, preserving her innocence.

Lucy stuck it out for two months but her fear of her employer, coupled with homesickness for Ireland, compelled her to send a telegram to Davey Williams, which read "Lucy coming home."

The adventure was not without its funny side, for a few weeks after arriving home, Darkie, who was supposed to be a tomcat, produced six kittens. Lucy and Lavinia had blamed the good English food for his increasing size! The kittens' arrival, however, did explain the very friendly tomcats!

After Birmingham, Lucy and Davey made a concerted effort to live a normal life and to Lavinia's surprise, even allowed her to have a pup. She called it Shep, fed it, walked it and loved it. The dog became her constant companion and, when the rows started again, she told Shep her troubles and cried into his fur. Many times she sneaked him up the stairs to her bedroom and let him snuggle down on the bed clothes beside her. He was her friend and her confidante, and for two years gave her the love and companionship she so much desired.

Then Lucy walked out and wouldn't let Lavinia bring the dog because she wasn't sure where they would live. They stayed away for three weeks, and when Lucy returned, as she always did, to the only place she could call home, a heartbroken Lavinia discovered that Shep had gone. She was told that, as there was no one to look after him, her stepfather had sent for the USPCA to take him away.

In the weeks that followed, Lavinia experienced a pain that hurt more than her bruises had ever hurt. She had learnt that bruises would fade and wounds would heal but she felt that this pain would never go away. It was her first real experience of the grief of loss. Shep was dead.

They moved house soon after and here things got steadily worse. The house itself was wrecked - furniture broken, doors kicked in and endless windows broken. By this time, Lavinia and her friend Betty were strong enough to carry the sash window frames to the glazier to have the broken frames of glass replaced. The house was always cold because there was always at least one broken window. The smell of stale beer and cigarette smoke filled the air and the walls were splattered with blood.

As Davey spiralled further and further into depression, the situation took a sinister turn. Lucy wakened one evening as a drunken Davey was stumbling around trying to get to bed and realised that there was a strange smell in the house. She went downstairs to investigate and to her horror discovered that Davey, perhaps in a drunken attempt to commit suicide, had turned on the gas to all the rings and to the oven. Lavinia awoke to her yelling,

"We're all gonna be killed! You'll not be happy till you've killed the lot of us!"

From that night on, a new fear was added to all the others, the fear of death. She used to dread the evenings for the violence they might bring but now she also feared the nights, afraid almost to go to sleep in case she would die in her sleep. She didn't know, of course, that God sent His angel to keep watch and someone in the house always woke up or the shilling in the meter ran out so her life was spared. God's plan for her was still to be fulfilled.

꩜

Chapter 9 ❧

FLYING ON BROKEN WINGS

"Would you be free from the burden of sin?
There's power in the blood of the Lamb."

The worshippers in the Percy Street Mission hall were singing
with great gusto, giving it their all and the strains of music that
floated out into the street found a response in the heart of the
twelve year old girl who was passing by.

"Oh I would love to go in there and be able to sing like
that," thought Lavinia but there was no one to go with her and
she was too shy to go on her own. She read the board outside
and noticed that the Girls' Auxiliary met there each Friday
night. By the following Friday she had persuaded Betty to go
with her and the two girls thoroughly enjoyed the activities.

The young woman, Nora Murphy, who led it, had a
daughter called Irene who was the same age as Lavinia and
they became friends. Irene invited Lavinia to her home, a very
different home to any Lavinia had known before - no fighting,
no threatening behaviour, no drinking, no fear. It was a lovely
peaceful place.

"If I ever have a home of my own," vowed Lavinia. "I want it to be like this one," and she made a conscious, firm decision that she would not marry a man who drank alcohol.

In the Murphys' home, Lavinia knew that she was close to what her heart had been seeking for some years now. They talked about being a Christian and when she stayed with them for weekends, they brought her to church on Sunday nights. When those who gave testimonies talked about sin, Lavinia recognised it and knew it was wrong for she had seen sin at work and she knew the awfulness in her own life and in the lives of others.

One night the Pastor spoke about coming to God. Lavinia desperately wanted to do that but didn't think that she was good enough to be a Christian, so she left to go home.

The longing kept coming back however and she suddenly stopped, turned to Betty and said, "Betty, I'm going back."

Pastor Porter was still in the church and was delighted when the two girls told him that they wanted to trust Jesus. He talked to them, prayed with them and in that little Mission Hall, they gave their lives to Jesus. The angel who kept watch flew in an instant into Heaven and soon the cry was ringing out.

"Rejoice, rejoice, two more children have come into the Kingdom! Rejoice!"

Back on earth it was scarcely any different, for Lavinia went skipping and dancing to her home that night. She felt different, a new person. It seemed as though God had come out of highest Heaven and actually jumped right into her heart. Every empty space inside was filled up in that moment.

She felt special, rich beyond measure - like a princess who had free access to all the resources of the King. For the first time she became Someone's daughter and took great delight in calling God her father. It really didn't matter any more what was going on outside, there was so much wonder inside that the pain and disappointment were overcome. She felt an instant bond with God, as though she had always known Him and had the sense that they were inseparable. She didn't come down to earth for six weeks and couldn't sleep at night for the joy.

Lucy's comment was not the most encouraging - "If you can keep it in this house, it'll be a miracle."

But now that she and God were together, Lavinia knew that even miracles were possible. She was soaring in her spirit - flying, maybe on broken wings, but still flying!

Chapter 10 🐦

APPOINTMENTS WITH GOD

"Bang! Bang! Bang!"

The reverent atmosphere of the Sunday service was broken by a loud commotion at the back of the building.

"Oi, open the door! Let me in!"

One of the deacons opened the church door and Davey staggered down the aisle to where Lavinia sat. He pulled her roughly by the hair and dragged her down the aisle after him, swearing and shouting loudly all the way. No one tried to stop him - it wasn't usual to interfere in what was seen as a domestic problem. Since Lavinia's conversion, Davey had found a new way to annoy Lavinia and, through her, to upset Lucy.

The folks in the church supported her in whatever way they could, loving her and praying for her but the whole issue of Lavinia's conversion and interest in spiritual matters was seen as a threat in the house. Each time someone gave her a Bible, Davey tore it up or burnt it. After this had happened a few times, Lavinia developed the habit of reading her Bible in the outside toilet! Sitting in that cold, uncomfortable place, she discovered that Jesus was building a mansion in Heaven - her own wonderful home - and that one day He would take her there. Thoughts of Heaven became very precious and remained so all her life. The idea that she would spend eternity in God's presence, worshipping Him, just thrilled her. She felt homesick for Heaven.

God's Word was a source of great comfort to her. She didn't understand all the words but she sensed that God could speak to her through the Bible and that amazed and delighted her. Another source of comfort to her was a little ten commandments bracelet. She wore it as often as possible and could glance down at the commandments on it when she wasn't allowed to read her Bible openly.

Lavinia had a strong desire to tell others about Jesus and used to go to the street corners where the young people congregated to preach to them. They got somewhat fed up with this twelve year old girl and would shout, "Here's Holy Mary!" when they saw her coming up the street. A few of them however, were persuaded to go to church and some later gave their lives to Jesus.

By Easter of the following year, Lucy had once more left Davey and gone to stay at Uncle Billy's house but Lavinia continued to go back to the Shankill Road to the meetings. She had since started attending The Church of God, Shankill Road, attracted once again by the singing and the fact that they had a tambourine band.

One evening, as she walked near her home on the way to the Easter Convention meeting, one of the neighbours stopped her.

"No one has seen your father for days and there's bottles of milk outside the door," she was told.

When she informed Lucy of this, her mother asked Davey's cousin to go with her to the house and he broke down the door. They found Davey lying dead on Lavinia's bed. He had taken an overdose.

Despite all he had put her through, Lucy became hysterical with grief and at the funeral a few days later, she fainted. For some time afterwards, she cried bitterly for the husband who had so ill-treated her. Theirs had been a strange relationship, a real love/hate relationship. Lavinia could only remember the hate and couldn't understand her mother's distress.

Their stay at Uncle Billy's was extended as a result of the police investigation into Davey's death and it was over a year before they were able to return home. Lucy had a steady job, as a result of which they were able to buy some second-hand furniture and Lavinia went back to sleep in her old room, in the very bed where her step-father had taken his own life.

It was at this more peaceful period in Lavinia's life that God took the opportunity to reveal Himself more deeply to her. She felt a strong call to pray and regularly woke at two o'clock in the morning, got out of bed to kneel on the cold oilcloth and spent the next two hours in prayer. She had no clock of her own so she used to carry the clock from the mantelpiece in the sitting room up to her bedroom, then quietly leave it back again before Lucy woke up. Despite not having an alarm, she always woke up. These hours were like appointments that God always kept and she didn't dare to break. She saw nothing unusual in what she was doing and in her naivety, assumed that all Christians did the same.

These were very special times, a bedrock of strength on which she could rest in the years to come. The Lord gave her a promise, "Delight yourself in the Lord and He will give you the desires of your heart."

She discovered that the more time she spent on her knees, the more delight she found. God just lit up her life, pouring in His peace and joy and comfort. She prayed that God would use her, but her strong will meant that she often cried tears of repentance for she could no longer live with sin. God was doing a work in her life, a spiritual building that she scarcely understood.

Lucy most certainly didn't understand it, for when she found out about Lavinia's middle-of-the-night prayer meetings, she was concerned for her daughter's sanity and took her to the doctor.

"She won't stop praying, Doctor, and I don't know what to do with her," was her complaint. The doctor had never had a problem like that before and had no answer for it. He simply tried to assure Lucy that it was just a passing phase, that she would get over it.

A phase? Would that all young Christians could go through a similar phase!

Chapter 11 ❧

A LITTLE BIT FURTHER

The 2 a.m. appointments with God were a foundation on which a life of service could be built.

Lavinia joined the tambourine band and six months later became its leader. She learned to play the guitar and was soon asked to sing solos or duets in various meetings. The Pastor and the people in the Shankill Road Church encouraged and supported this new convert, seeing the potential in her and a determination to rise above the awful circumstances of her life. There were tears in the eyes of many as they listened for the first time to this young girl and her friend Kathleen singing "Whispering Hope", her face aglow with the wonder of the hope she had discovered since she had met Jesus. Young as they were, she and her friend often prayed and fasted before a singing engagement. They were taught that service rendered in their own strength, that did not depend on God's Holy Spirit for power, was empty and futile.

Betty, who used to accompany Lavinia to have panes of glass replaced, now accompanied her to sing at Gospel services.

On one occasion the two girls travelled to Greenisland by bus and train to sing in a meeting. The sermon that evening was of particular significance to Lavinia. The preacher spoke of Jesus in Gethesemane and quoted the verse -

"Jesus went a little bit further."

Lavinia determined there and then that each time Jesus went on a little bit further in her life, she would follow in obedience to him.

Obedience to Jesus meant saying "Yes" when asked to sing at cottage meetings and in churches; saying "Yes" when asked to give her testimony at open airs in front of Belfast City Hall; saying "Yes" when her pastor lent her books to read and encouraged her to study; saying "Yes" to the challenge presented to her in sermons preached by Pastor McConnell, a young pastor from the Whitewell church who brought to life the characters of the Old Testament; saying "Yes" when a stranger arrived on the doorstep, begging her to sing at a meeting that night as his booked singer had let him down and someone had told him about a wee girl on the Shankill Road who would take her place; saying "Yes" when asked to preach her first sermon at a Youth Rally at the age of fourteen! She had little knowledge of the Bible and no knowledge of theology so she preached on the only two things she was sure of - the Good Shepherd and Heaven.

Lavinia learnt major lessons from the folks who gathered to various meetings in the church, lessons about worship, commitment and honesty, lessons that would form the basis of her own response to the God who had served her. She watched while people worshipped and was moved to see grown men and women unashamedly sing hymns about Jesus and His cross, with tears rolling down their faces, focused totally on the Lord, oblivious to all around them. In later life she would attend seminars on worship, given by some of the greatest worship leaders of our time but she learnt no more from them than she had already learnt from observing the faces of these ordinary people at worship.

She was there when, now and again, the Holy Spirit would descend on a meeting and these same men and women would go forward to rededicate their lives to God, this time crying tears of repentance. Their awareness of sin in their lives and their willingness to admit to it honestly in front of their friends impressed Lavinia greatly. Never again would she be among people who were so honest. She sought to be like them and asked Pastor Forsythe for advice,

"How often do I need to rededicate my life to the Lord?"

"Every day," was his reply.

Lucy didn't know what to make of her daughter. While not being totally happy about her interest in spiritual things, she wasn't hostile and Lavinia was given much more freedom to attend meetings whenever she wanted. Only one thing really bothered Lucy - in her experience, a church service that began at eight should be all over by nine. In Lavinia's church, however, if the Spirit moved, the people didn't go home but stayed for a couple of hours, worshipping and praying. Lucy felt sure that Lavinia must be up to something suspicious on these occasions and was ready with a hiding when she eventually returned late at night. When faced with a decision between escaping a hiding or receiving a blessing, for Lavinia there was simply no choice. The blessing won every time.

Eventually Lavinia persuaded Lucy that the only way to find out whether or not she was telling the truth was to go to church herself. Lucy had been greatly impressed by the support given to both of them by the church after Davey's death. It had been largely due to the intervention of Mr. Arnott, the church solicitor, that Lucy had been allowed to take possession of Davey's house and she had never forgotten his kindness. So she agreed to give it a try and sometime later made a commitment to Jesus. Her faith might have been weak and faltering but it was real, so real that on more than one occasion, those who attended the prayer meetings were astounded to hear Lucy praying fervently for her Catholic neighbours.

❧

Chapter 12 ❧

ROMANCE AND REVIVAL

Valerie nudged Lavinia as the two girls stood watching the boys playing football and giggling together at the edge of the playground.

"Go on, tell me - who do you fancy?"

Lavinia laughed and leaned forward to whisper in her friend's ear.

"The dark fella, with the black hair. Aye, he's not bad - nice brown eyes. He could take me out anytime!"

The two girls giggled again then Lavinia said somewhat sadly, "But sure he'd never notice the likes of us. He's two years older than us."

With that, the girls went on their way. They didn't notice, of course, that the angel who watched gave a little giggle too. He knew something they didn't!

The young man in question, Robin Abrol, whom Lavinia thought was the most handsome boy in the school, had acquired his swarthy skin, dark hair and brown eyes from his Indian ancestry. His parents owned a shop in the area and

Lavinia couldn't see how there was any chance of meeting him and getting to know him better. What she didn't realise was that the young man from the church who was teaching her to play the guitar was Robin's brother. Lavinia was delighted to catch sight of Robin on one of the occasions when she had to call at his brother's house and was even more delighted when his brother managed to persuade Robin to go to church.

That Sunday evening service was a turning point in Robin's life. When Tom Pinkerton began to preach, Robin felt that this preacher knew everything about him and was speaking only to him. So convinced was he of this that he went to him afterwards to question him, "Has my brother been talking to you about me?"

"No," Tom replied, "what makes you think that?"

The conversation that followed ended with Robin giving his life to the Lord.

The following Tuesday evening was a Bible study. The new convert was there and Lavinia took the chance to tell him how wonderful she thought it was that he had become a Christian. They chatted for a while, then Robin, who was quite taken with this pretty girl who was so friendly, asked her if he could walk her home.

Romance blossomed in the months that followed. Robin, who was a telephone engineer apprentice, went to Lavinia's house every evening after work. Their dates usually consisted of going to meetings, then calling into Beattie's or The Eagle for a fish supper on the way home.

Lucy was greatly encouraged by the romance - maybe her daughter was quite normal after all! Having a boyfriend was something Lucy could relate to easily and she took Robin to her heart, delighted to be able to cook for a man once again. One of her favourite dishes was potatoes and sausages, presented in a shape that looked like a wigwam - a huge sloping pile of potatoes with sausages sticking out of the top of the heap. One of the sausages came to a sorry end - Robin was tucking into his dinner one evening when a furry paw curled round the edge of the table, searched frantically till it found a plate and swiftly removed a sausage. The horrified Robin watched helplessly as his sausage disappeared out of the door in Methuselah's mouth! Lucy and Lavinia laughed so much they could hardly finish off their meal.

One of her teatime favourites also presented Robin with a problem. Lucy had made banana sandwiches but as Robin took his first bite, his face froze in horror and he began to think that Lucy was not as fond of him as she made out. Lavinia sensed that something was wrong and looked enquiringly at him.

"There's glass in it," he muttered out of the side of his mouth, torn between the desire to spit it out and the equally strong desire not to offend Lucy. Lavinia started to laugh, "Don't be daft. She's put sugar in it!"

He soon got used to sugar in sandwiches and a cat that stole sausages and he even got used to Lucy's early warning system. When Robin brought Lavinia home each evening they used to linger in the hallway, reluctant to be parted. When Lucy thought they had lingered long enough she found yet another use for milk bottles and would rattle them together as she went to the door calling out, "I'm coming. Isn't it time you were going home, son?"

At one of the numerous meetings attended by Lavinia and Robin, they met Maisie, who had been in the same class as Lavinia and had also left on the same day. In the first year of their secondary schooling, Lucy had met Maisie's mother at one of the school functions and they recognised one another. The last time they had spoken had been in the hospital when both baby girls had almost died. The girls had been amused to discover that they had "known" each other all those years ago.

Lavinia had very reluctantly left school the day after her fifteenth birthday. Secondary school had proved to be much more of a success than primary school had been. She had been able to stay in the one school all the time, had become involved in the choir and in drama and loved it so much that she cried when she had to leave.

She went to work in Christie's wallpaper shop where her natural creativity meant that she was rather good at helping people to match wallpaper and paint. After a year there, she heard that the Government had introduced a school grant which she realised could be used to help her return to school. She pestered Lucy until she agreed to let her go back to secondary school for another year. Poor Lucy had such a difficult job trying to understand this strange daughter of hers!

"Guess what, Maisie - I'm going back to school in September," said Lavinia excitedly.

"I don't believe you! Well, what do you know, I'm going back too!"

Maisie had also become a Christian and the two of them formed a firm friendship that has lasted for the rest of their lives. They joined the Scripture Union in school, joining forces with a Christian teacher, Pearl McComb. The Lord blessed and the three of them saw what was almost a mini revival in the school that year. Numbers swelled in the Scripture Union and pupils often stopped Lavinia in the corridor to ask her how they could become Christians. An appointment would be set up for lunch time and one more child would enter the Kingdom.

These new converts were keen to grow and readily agreed when Lavinia suggested attending Torchbearer Rallies at lunchtime.

"But how will we get there?" they asked

"We'll get a bus there and back," replied Lavinia.

The more fearful and law-abiding among them questioned the wisdom of this adventure.

"But Lavinia, we'll never make it back in time. If we're late for school in the afternoon we'll get caned."

"Never mind," Lavinia encouraged them, "sure doesn't it say in the Bible that we are to suffer for Jesus? He suffered enough for us, what's a caning compared to that?"

So the whole group regularly got the bus to the Rally, enjoyed the meeting, got the bus back to school and got caned or slippered for being late!

Chapter 13 ❧

STONES, BOMBS AND UMBRELLAS

All this time, while there was romance in the air and revival in the school, there was also rioting in the streets. Civil Rights marches of the early sixties led to what has now become known as "The Troubles". Catholics and Protestants who had lived peaceably enough in adjacent streets for many years, began to look on each other as enemies. Crowds gathered on the street corners each evening and name calling soon progressed to stone throwing which in turn led to petrol bombing. The Shankill Road was the scene of some of the bitterest feeling and the fiercest fighting.

So life changed once again for Lavinia. Where once the fighting had taken place inside the house, now the fighting took place in the street outside. She came to dread the nightly call to arms - the banging of dustbin lids. The noise was incredible - the yelling, the thuds of stones again walls and doors, the smash of a petrol bomb as it landed in the street, the screaming of sirens as police cars and fire engines moved into position. As the time went on and the fighting got worse, these sounds were often punctuated by the sharp cracks of shots being fired. Lavinia was afraid to be left on her own in the house at night.

One evening in the early days, the police shouted for people to help them and Lucy ran out to answer the call without a thought for her own safety and without considering how her involvement might damage her testimony. The call from her past proved to be stronger than her more recent call to love and reconciliation and soon she was heavily involved, collecting stones in the deep pocket of her apron for the men to throw in the evenings. She was so good at it that she earned the title "the best stone carrier in the Shankill". She learned how to make petrol bombs and joined a group of women who spent hours filling milk bottles with petrol and sugar and stuffing rags in the tops. It all answered a need in Lucy - a need to belong, to be part of a community, a need to fight for something she considered to be worthwhile, a need to be wanted and appreciated. She tried to persuade Lavinia to help her and couldn't understand why her daughter would only very reluctantly agree to collect milk bottles for her and that only after the threat of a hiding. For the next few years no milkman in the surrounding streets ever got his empty bottles returned!

Lucy was a strange mixture of aggression and compassion, for one night she arrived home from the riots with her apron pocket holding, not a collection of stones, but a cat! It had got caught up in the fighting and Lucy had taken pity on it and brought it home. It was named Methuselah, because he looked like an old cat and he lived up to his name, since he was around for many years afterwards. This was the same Methuselah who liked sausages so much that he would try to steal them from the dinner table.

The house often seemed to be a meeting place for strange men. At the time Lavinia thought that Lucy had lots of boyfriends but many years later discovered that her mother had been running a safe house for men caught up in the troubles. Her sense of adventure and her deep seated need to be involved seem to have overcome any thought she might have had of the possible consequences for herself and for Lavinia if she was caught.

As Lucy began staying out later and later, Lavinia, Robin and Uncle Billy became more and more concerned for her safety and spent many nights searching the streets, trying to find Lucy and bring her home. It was no easy task, as Robin and Uncle Billy discovered one night.

"I do wish Mammy would hurry up and come home," said Lavinia, as she returned from the front door where, once again, she had been looking out to see if Lucy was anywhere nearby.

"Do you want me to try and find her?" asked Robin, who knew that she wouldn't be content until Lucy was back safely.

"Would you, Robin? Take Uncle Billy with you. He might know where to look for her."

Soon afterwards Robin and Uncle Billy set off for Peter's Hill, dodging their way through the many parked landrovers that spoke of a heavy police presence in the area. As they emerged at the back of a large group of police in riot gear, Uncle Billy spied Lucy among a crowd on the street corner.

"There she is!" he shouted. Suddenly a cry of "Charge!" went up from the police officer in charge and Robin and Uncle Billy saw the policemen hold out their batons at the ready and realised that they were going to try and disperse the very crowd in which Lucy was standing. They stood rooted to the spot in horror as the large group of policemen charged down the street. The people in the crowd at the corner immediately began to run away, all except for one lone figure, who, raising her umbrella like a baton, charged back towards the police. The policemen saw this wild woman from the Shankill coming in their direction, frantically waving her umbrella and parted ranks. Lucy ran through them unscathed, then proceeded to launch an attack on a policeman whom she found beating a rioter with his baton. Just as Uncle Billy ran over to pull her away, she took her umbrella and stuck it where no umbrella should ever have been stuck. The enraged policeman turned round, saw Uncle Billy and hit him!

Billy went back to Robin, holding his aching shoulder.

"Let's leave her - she's gonna have us killed."

These were perilous times on the Shankill Road but still the angel watched and while she rested under the shadow of the Almighty, no stone or petrol bomb or bullet could harm Lavinia.

Chapter 14 〜

THE GOD OF MIRACLES

Lavinia met the God of miracles very early in her Christian life. She came to Him with some great advantages - no one ever told her that God didn't do miracles, she had a simple faith that believed what the Bible said: she had nothing to unlearn - no prior "knowledge", no misconceptions. She had no doubt that if a miracle was needed, then God could do it. She had seen sick people in her church go to the front to ask for prayer and had seen these same people praise God for their healing.

When Lavinia developed a cyst on the side of her face, the doctor wanted to send her to the hospital to have it cut out but she thought it would be a lot easier just to go to the elders and ask them to pray for her. So next time that opportunity was given at the end of the meeting for those who wanted prayer for healing to raise their hands, Lavinia's was the first hand to be raised. The elders gathered round to anoint her with oil and prayed that God would heal her. By the time the letter came from the hospital confirming the appointment, the cyst had gone.

The timing of the miracles was not always so convenient however, as Lavinia learned in rather an amusing incident that taught her to be wise about exactly when and where she prayed for a 'miracle'. Soon after giving her life to Jesus, Lavinia heard in her church about being filled with the Holy Spirit and about a new language that was sometimes given as a gift of the Spirit. She was eager to learn all she could so she asked for the elders to lay hands on her, and to her amazement she found that she could speak in this new language.

She could hardly wait to get to school the next day to tell her friend Maisie all about it and soon Maisie was just as eager to receive the gift as Lavinia had been. The two girls were still talking about it as the class began to settle for an English period, reading a novel around the class.

"Quick, Lavinia, before she starts, pray for me now," Maisie begged. Lavinia gave no thought to the consequences of such a prayer but quickly laid her hand on her friend. As she prayed, Maisie began to shake and quickly mutter words. She tried to stop shaking and couldn't, she tried to stop praying aloud and couldn't.

"Now Maisie, it's your turn," the teacher announced, "just continue reading the next paragraph."

Lavinia looked at Maisie encouragingly and showed her where to read, but Maisie couldn't even get the first word out.

"Lavinia, what's wrong with Maisie?" asked the teacher.

It was difficult to know what to say in the circumstances and in the end Lavinia just replied, "Ah she's not herself, Miss."

Maisie continued to shake helplessly and the teacher assumed that she was feeling unwell.

"Change places girls, and let Maisie sit beside the radiator. The heat will make her feel better."

Maisie couldn't eat her lunch and on her way home from school, had to get someone else to buy her bus ticket for her.

"Oh dear," thought Lavinia., "I know what to say to make the miracle happen but I should have found out how to make it stop!"

There are times when people ask for prayer for healing and the healing comes but it is difficult to be sure that the healing is the direct result of the prayer. Those who are sceptical of healing are inclined to dismiss it by saying that the sick person would get better anyway, that the healing is just a natural process. At other times, healing is so immediate and unexpected and medically so well documented, that no other explanation can be given but that a miracle has taken place.

Such an incident occurred when Lavinia was seventeen.

"What's the matter with you?" Lucy asked. "You don't look a bit well and you've been mopin' around the house for days."

"I feel sick all the time," replied Lavinia wearily, "And I'm so tired I could sleep for a week."

Lucy came over to take a closer look and her eyes widened when she looked into Lavinia's face.

"Your eyes are all yella, Lavinia. Come on, get your coat, we're goin' to see the doctor. Here, wait a minute, them doctors are always askin' for samples. Get a bottle and bring a sample with you, it'll save you doin' it down there."

Lucy was right - the doctor did ask for a sample and on seeing its brown colour, immediately realised that she was very sick indeed. Lavinia was jaundiced as a result of hepatitis. When the doctor told them that she would have to go into Purdysburn Hospital for treatment, Lucy began to cry.

"Oh no Doctor, not into hospital. I'll not let you put her into hospital."

Like many other people at that time, Lucy had a real fear of hospitals. She felt that too many people, who went in for treatment, never came out again.

The doctor couldn't admit Lavinia without her mother's consent but made it very clear that if she insisted on nursing her at home, he would not be held responsible for the outcome.

On the way home, Lucy began to feel guilty about the decision she had made and in an attempt to reassure her, Lavinia told her that there were elders in her church who prayed for people and they got healed. Lucy wasn't too convinced about the whole idea but reluctantly agreed to let the elders visit Lavinia at home.

The visit was quickly arranged and Pastor Forsythe came with some of the elders, laid hands on Lavinia, anointed her with oil and prayed for her. Lavinia had no doubt that she was healed and almost immediately began to feel less nauseous and less tired and asked for a plate of chips to eat. Lucy brought another sample to the doctor the next day. He was dumbfounded when he saw the clear sample - the hepatitis had gone! The jaundice left her eyes and her appetite returned but, although Lavinia and Lucy knew that she was better, others were not so easily convinced. The school insisted that she stay off for the normal period of six weeks and the library collected and burned her books as a precautionary measure against infection. Neither of these circumstances pleased Lavinia - not only was she forced to stay at home from her beloved school but she didn't even have a book to read!

Lavinia's miraculous healing didn't even surprise her. If she asked God to heal her, she just took it for granted that He would answer her - she took God at His word. In later years, she would look back on this period of her life and say, "I wish I could have bottled what I had then."

With prescriptions costing two shillings and sixpence, she reckoned that it was cheaper to pray - and for once, Lucy agreed with her!

Chapter 15 ❧

WEDDING PLANS

Two dark heads were bent in concentration over the tray of rings.

"Can I choose any of these?" asked Lavinia.

"Yes, any one at all," was the reply.

This was such a special moment. Although Lavinia was only seventeen and still at school, she and Robin had decided to go ahead with their engagement, and had come into the city centre to choose a ring. It had all been so perfect. They spent some time looking in the window at all the magnificent engagement rings, then went in to Adlestones shop with its hushed atmosphere and deep pile carpet. The assistant treated them like royalty, calling them 'Sir' and 'Madam' and ushered them into a little private room where they could make their choice. It all felt a bit like being in a fairytale.

Eventually Lavinia chose a ring with three diamonds and it was placed in one of the jeweller's ring boxes. They announced their engagement on the 27th November 1968 and set their wedding date for the following year. Both families were happy and treated them to special meals as a celebration of their engagement. Lavinia wore her engagement ring on a chain around her neck at school and just knowing it was there caused a bubble of excitement inside her.

The months passed in a blur of school lessons, services and wedding preparations until, before she knew it, Lavinia was approaching both the end of her school career and her eighteenth birthday. Robin's present of a beautiful white broderie anglaise dress brought cries of delight from Lavinia and Lucy.

"So where do you want to go for your birthday?" he asked. "What about a nice, fancy restaurant - splash out a bit?"

"Do you know what I'd really like to do?" came the reply. "I'd like to go to a good long meeting."

It was an unusual way to celebrate a birthday but the birthday girl got her wish. A Belfast Telegraph was bought and they searched the church news page for a suitable 'good long meeting'. Lavinia was particularly anxious that it should be long, so that she would be allowed to stay out until eleven o'clock. They decided in the end to go to a meeting in the Assemblies of God in the Ardoyne, and Lavinia set out in her new white dress and a matching white bow in her hair, happier to spend her birthday in a meeting than in a big city restaurant.

As the date for their wedding, 17th November, drew nearer, Lavinia experienced mixed emotions. Lucy suddenly became aware of how much Lavinia's marriage would change her life and often Lavinia would come in to find her sitting with her head in her hands.

"What'll I do? What'll I do?" she would cry.

In the face of Lucy's distress, Lavinia found it difficult to be as outwardly happy as she felt inwardly. She was looking forward so much to setting up home in her own wee house, a house that would be filled with pretty things, where the furniture wouldn't be used as firewood or the dishes be used as missiles, a house that would always be warm and smell sweet. She was looking forward to getting away from the troubles - the house they had bought in Brookmount Street, though still in the Shankill, was in a safer area. Lavinia was looking forward to running her own life - having the freedom to stay out late any

Lavinia and Robin on the 'Big Day'.

night she wanted to and the financial security to buy biscuits every day of the week!

In the weeks before the wedding, Robin's parents bought them some furniture for the house and the young couple, who had saved hard all year and now had £99 in the bank, ordered wedding cars and flowers and arranged for a wedding reception to take place in the church hall. The marriage ceremony itself had to take place in the Whitewell Church, as their own church wasn't licensed for marriage. They arranged to spend a week on honeymoon in a house in Millisle, a seaside resort not far from Belfast.

So everything was in order for the big day - well almost everything! Lavinia's idea of a perfect marriage was a little different to most people's, so a few weeks before the wedding took place she had a few very important requests for Robin.

"When we're married, can we have a dog?"

"Yes, we can have a dog."

Lavinia pressed on with the next question.

"And can we have a cat as well?"

"Yes alright, a cat as well."

Lavinia gave her young fiancé her most winning smile.

"And can we have six children too?"

"Six children, sure, why not?"

That reply, spoken with all the carefree ignorance of youth, set the pattern for the early years of their marriage. He might not have agreed so readily if he had known what those years would bring.

Chapter 16 ❧

CATREEN

Marriage could sometimes be likened to building a jigsaw with pieces that don't quite fit properly. For some couples all that is required to complete the picture is a gentle jiggling of the pieces but for others, major adjustments are required.

For the newly married Mr and Mrs Abrol, some major adjustments had to be made. Robin's family had never kept animals but within a month, a cat had been procured from the Cat Protection League and a poodle puppy called Kelly, had also joined the family.

Lavinia had to learn how to cook and her first culinary attempts were far from perfect. Potatoes that should have been well cooked, that looked perfect on the outside, turned out to be like rocks on the inside.

They both had to get used, not only to the fundamental differences in a man and a woman but also to the individual differences in their personalities. Robin was quiet and contemplative, while Lavinia was fiery and hot-headed. She was quick to tell others about Jesus, quick to minister to those in need but also quick to answer back and to confront. She went into marriage with a strongly held determination that she would not be treated the way her mother had been and this determination was the cause of her quick reaction to even the slightest criticism.

One warm day early on in the marriage, Lavinia spent most of the afternoon making a lovely dinner for Robin. She had a fire on to give a cosy atmosphere in the house. Robin, meanwhile, had worked hard all day and was feeling hot and sticky when he arrived home. His first words on walking into the house were a mild enough criticism, "Oh, you haven't got a hot dinner on a night like that?"

Mild it may have been, but it was enough to set Lavinia's blood boiling. She got up from her place, snatched his dinner from the table and scraped it into the fire.

"Well now you don't have to eat it!" she announced. For the next couple of days there was an uneasy tension in the house but they were young and in love and soon made up their quarrel. As the weeks and months went by, readjustments were made until Robin and Lavinia were fairly comfortable living with each other.

The cat and the dog settled in very quickly and Lavinia was convinced that everything was going according to plan when she went to the doctor in April and he confirmed that she was going to have a baby. She hugged the secret to herself all the way home from the surgery. She felt so special.

"Just imagine!" she thought. "I'm going to be a mammy!"

Her excited thoughts tumbled about inside her head - how would she tell Robin? What would her mother think? Where would the baby sleep? What would the baby look like? What would it feel like to hold a child in her arms?

In the weeks that followed, Robin and she made plans for this new little life. They bought a big pram, a cot, nappies and baby clothes. Lavinia was happier than she had ever been before. She had a feeling that this baby would be a girl and bought pink and white wool from which she painstakingly crocheted a baby shawl. She sat contentedly day after day, praying for the child as she crocheted. As she washed and cleaned and cooked, she sang songs of praise and such was the joy in her heart that it seemed that the colours all around her were brighter and the days sunnier.

Excitement mounted as the due date in December approached but the excitement turned to worry when the baby was a week overdue and seemed to have stopped moving.

The Practice Nurse tried to reassure her when she examined her and failed to find a heartbeat with the foetal stethoscope.

"Don't be too concerned, Mrs Abrol, sometimes we can't find a heartbeat because of the way the baby's lying."

The nurse sent her on to the Royal Maternity Hospital where the doctors had a machine for listening to the foetal heartbeat but though they tried many times, they also failed to find a heartbeat.

"We're really very sorry," they said at last.

Lavinia had made no preparations for a time like this. She felt bewildered and lost and very scared.

"What will I do?" she enquired.

The doctor explained that she would have to go through a normal delivery. Lavinia assumed that they would take her into the hospital and asked if she should fetch her case but they told her that they were too busy just then and sent her home.

She went home in a daze wondering how she would tell Robin that her baby was dead when she herself could hardly take it in. Each time she moved the baby seemed to move too and her heart would beat a little faster - maybe, somehow the doctors might have been wrong. Her friends and neighbours met her in the street and she didn't know how to answer when they asked her how she was.

When she was finally admitted to hospital, she was put on a drip to start labour. The next twenty-four hours felt like a nightmare. She knew that she was carrying death inside her and that knowledge had an awful effect on her. It was although she was taking part in an execution.

As she walked the corridor outside the labour ward, a mixture of fear and pain causing her stomach to churn, she knew a terrible sense of isolation. She thought that she was the only woman ever to have a dead baby. She had never heard of miscarriage or stillbirth and her lack of knowledge contributed greatly to the sense that she was no longer in control. She wished she could stop this dreadful thing that had happened to her but stopping was not an option and each contraction drove her on relentlessly to its conclusion. Although someone was with her all the time, Lavinia felt so alone. No one could really help her, no one could have this baby for her.

It took a long time, twenty-four hours, but at last the baby was delivered. This young mother heard no longed for first cry, only silence. A nurse wrapped the little baby in a green sheet and carried it away. As Lavinia watched, she caught a quick glimpse of dark hair peeping out from the edge of the sheet. She thought her heart would break.

Some time later, back on the ward, she woke from sleep and spoke to the nurse who was attending her.

"Did I have a baby?"

"Yes," replied the nurse.

"What was it?"

"A girl."

"What weight was she?"

"Seven pounds and nine ounces."

"Was the baby dead?"

"Yes. I'm sorry."

"Can I see her?"

"No, that wouldn't be a good idea. Your baby has been dead for over a week."

Lavinia longed to see her daughter but when she asked the doctor, he also said no.

When it became obvious to her that no-one was prepared to let her see her baby, Lavinia began to think there must have been something terribly wrong with her child - maybe she had given birth to some sort of monster. These fears subsided a little when she met one of the nurses who had actually seen her and was able to tell her that the baby had long fingers and dark hair that was long enough to tie back with a bow. Those two facts were the only things that she would ever know of the little girl who would have been Lavinia Catreen.

On the wall of the side ward where she had been put to save her the distress of seeing other mothers with their babies, there was a picture of a scene by a riverside. A tree grew beside the river and its branches leaned out over the water. The scene reminded Lavinia of a nursery rhyme.

"Hush a bye baby
On the tree top
When the wind blows
The cradle will rock
When the bough breaks
The cradle will fall
Down will come baby
Cradle and all."

For Lavinia, the bough had been broken. Part of her had died and would never come alive again. Heaven had been special to her before but now she was drawn to it even more for she knew that her daughter was there and that one day they would be reunited.

Family and friends came to visit her, to offer sympathy and support but it was obvious that they all felt uncomfortable and no-one knew what to say. They avoided the subject that Lavinia most needed to talk about - the death of her baby. One visitor, however, brought a book which did help her. Her pastor's wife, Grace Forsythe lent her Amy Carmichael's story "Mamosa". It told of a young woman who had lost babies too and Lavinia found one of her prayers very helpful. When these dark days came, she used to tell God:

"I'm not offended with you. I don't know why it happened but I don't blame you."

Lavinia determined to make this her prayer as well.

In the two days following the birth, while Lavinia recovered in hospital, Robin and Lucy had their own hard things to face. Robin was asked if he wanted to arrange the burial of the baby but he was so numb with grief that he didn't know what to say. He was relieved when they assured him that the hospital would take care of it but he never thought to ask how they would do so. This meant that neither Robin nor Lavinia knew if the baby had been cremated or buried and had no opportunity to say goodbye properly. Robin also had to go and register a death instead of a birth and that was a very difficult experience.

Lucy was very distressed by it all and didn't have the strong faith of her daughter to help her cope. She needed to do something and thought that she could best help Lavinia by removing all the items they had gathered up for the baby and having the house clean and tidy for her. So Lavinia returned home on the 22nd December to a house that had no reminders of her pregnancy - it was as though it had never happened. Although Lucy meant well, the removal of the pram and the baby clothes only served to underline the feeling of unreality which Lavinia had. The doctor's last words on discharging her from hospital were along the same lines,

"Go home and forget all about it - you're young enough to have more children."

She moved through that Christmas time in a world of pain and grief. She found it impossible to celebrate the birth of a Child when she had just lost her own. Carols made her cry and fairy lights and tinsel seemed so out of place. She heard people telling her to stop crying and because she didn't know what else to do, she tried to stop the tears, tried to carry on as if life was normal, tried not to turn away when she saw someone else with a baby. She went back to church again and eventually managed to sing the hymns without breaking down. She went back to work, starting a new job where no-one knew what had happened. The girls who worked with her were friendly and soon tried to get to know her by asking the usual questions. The inevitable happened and someone asked,

"Have you any children?"

In that moment, the dam of bottled up grief just broke and she ran from the room in floods of tears. She cried for a long time and somehow the tears brought a measure of relief from the pain and released her from the terrible pressure of being brave.

She found a little comfort too one day when she came across the shawl she had so lovingly crocheted for her baby. It had escaped Lucy's clear-out because Lavinia had hidden it away in a drawer. As she took it out and wept over it, she sensed deep within her some instinct that told her to keep the little shawl, that in later years it would be good to look at it and think of Catreen, that it would somehow be very important to make a memory.

And the angels still kept watch and Jesus still walked with her, closer in her grief than He had ever been before and slowly, very slowly her heart began to heal.

Chapter 17 ❧

On The Road

Jack Fisher smiled when he heard the sound of singing as he opened the church door. He was a well-loved deacon in the church and had come early to prepare for the service. The music grew louder as he climbed the stairs to the little meeting hall where they were held and he recognised the voices. Robin and Lavinia and their friends were having a practice. He quietly slipped in to the back of the church, where he stood listening for a moment or two. All at once he became aware that this was no ordinary practice for the presence of the Lord so filled the place that he felt he couldn't remain there but had to go back outside again.

The singing group grew out of a shared pain. Lavinia had lost her baby and when she met up with Maisie Hill again, she discovered that Maisie had recently lost her mother. Maisie had also been married to Sammy and the two couples began to meet regularly. They shared a love for singing and soon decided to form a little group with two others, Glynn and Karen from the Shankill Church. After a while, Robin's brother, Roger joined them too. Their name, The Persuaders, was taken from a verse in the Bible, found by Robin, "Knowing the terror of the Lord, we persuade men."

So they committed themselves to regular practice, learning new songs, trying out different accompaniments, working on the harmonies, seeking to ensure that what they sang would bring glory to God. They spent much time in prayer, aware that the hours of practice would be worthless if God's Spirit didn't anoint their songs, and God honoured and blessed them. Their practices often turned into real worship times, moments when God came among them to make His presence felt. Jack Fisher walked in on such a moment. On another occasion, during a worship time following the practice, Lavinia began to sing one of her favourite hymns. When she reached the third verse,

"My sin, Oh the bliss of this glorious thought
My sin, not in part but the whole,
Is nailed to His cross and I bear it no more
Praise the Lord, Praise the Lord, Oh my soul."

God's Spirit came in such power that some of the group fell to their knees in worship and the others moved to the walls for support. That song would always be special to Lavinia.

The singing and the worship helped to heal the heartache felt by both Maisie and Lavinia, so that the years following the loss of little Catreen were years of great joy and fellowship. As the wider Christian community began to hear of them, bookings started to come in from all over the country. Such was their determination to serve the Lord that they gave little thought to the potential dangers of a life "on the road". By this stage in her life, Lavinia had come to understand that God had commanded His angels to watch over her and she never doubted that He would provide all the protection she needed.

The early seventies were the years of the riots, fierce street fighting that took place in many areas of Northern Ireland, including the Shankill Road. It would have been easy and possibly even sensible to phone and cancel arrangements when the rioting was at its height but they would simply ask God to put His angel on the bonnet of the car and then set out for their destination. Lavinia would travel without fear, safe in the knowledge that God's mighty angel would forge a safe path for them through the dangerous streets.

One evening they had to go down the Falls Road, past a notorious area nicknamed Hijackers' Corner. As they approached, they could hear a terrible noise and realised that a riot was in progress. There was no other way to their engagement, so they wound down all their windows and the rioters were treated to the sound of the Persuaders belting out into the crowd at the top of their voices, the chorus, "God's not dead. No, He's alive!".

They were so startled that they stopped rioting just long enough to let the car race through. The sounds of stone throwing and glass breaking and the thump of petrol bombs exploding followed them down the street.

Their engagements often brought them to other troubled areas of Northern Ireland but they paid little heed to the danger, trusting that God would keep them safe. The week after they had sung in an Orange Hall in Markethill, gunmen broke into that same hall and shot dead five people. During these dark days in the Province, many others were murdered in that area around Armagh, close to the border with the Republic of Ireland. They were killed by men of violence, often in the name of religion, a religion of hatred and bitterness.

Thank God there were men and women like "The Persuaders", who were willing to risk their lives to sing of a true religion, a religion of love and forgiveness.

The God of miracles, whom Lavinia had come to know more and more, revealed His miraculous power in many of these situations, one of which came about as a direct result of the poor condition of their car. None of them could afford to buy a good car - in fact the evangelist Val English used to introduce them as "the group whose car goes on prayer and elastic". They set out to this particular engagement in a church near Armagh, knowing that their car might not make it and sure enough, the car broke down in a really bad area. The men got out to look under the bonnet but neither of them was a mechanic, so looking was all they were able to do. They returned to their seats in the car, conscious that time was racing on and the meeting would soon be starting. Sammy said "We'd better pray."

The four of them bowed their heads and soon after they began to pray, there was a knock at the window. Maisie was afraid to open her eyes convinced that if she did, she would see a terrorist with a mask and a gun. Sammy had more courage than his wife and wound down the window. As he talked to the man who stood outside, the group realised that this was no gunman but the Lord's own miraculous provision in the form of a mechanic who "just happened" to be passing by! He was able, not only to diagnose the problem, but also to tow them to their meeting and even managed to get them there on time.

The car featured in another incident that took place in Lisburn. The group parked the car, unloaded the guitars and amplifiers and began carrying them up into the hall. When they had returned to bring in the rest of the equipment, the car had gone.

"Someone's taken the car."

"No they haven't - look - oh my goodness."

"Catch it somebody! Quick!"

The cause of all their consternation was quietly rolling down the hill, gaining speed as it went along. They could only watch, frozen and unbelieving, as it careered towards the large plate glass window of a furniture shop. But God reached down His strong right arm and the car came to a halt just inches from the window. They all breathed a sigh of relief, said a prayer of thanks and retrieved the car, parking it this time where the faulty hand-brake wouldn't slip.

One of the most amazing escapes that Lavinia experienced took place not when she was with the group but when she was with a girl from work who had agreed to go with her to hear Leslie Hale preach. The two young women got a taxi home and they had arranged to drop Lavinia's friend off first at a garage on the main Shankill road, where she was to meet her boyfriend who was working there. At the last minute the taxi driver changed the plan and stopped instead at the top of Brookmount Street where Robin and Lavinia lived.

Just before Lavinia got out, there was a tremendous explosion about thirty feet away. The taxi was lifted right up into the air by the blast then slammed down violently and all of them were deafened by the noise. For a moment after the bomb exploded they couldn't see anything because of the dust cloud that rose up in front of them, then when the dust settled, they realised that the Four Step Inn had been blown up. The street was covered in chunks of masonry, pieces of broken glass, twisted metal and the remains of chairs and tables from the pub. For a moment there was an unearthly silence, then the screams began. Lavinia's friend was in hysterics, convinced that her boyfriend must be dead as the garage where he worked was next door to the Four Step Inn. She opened the taxi door and ran off towards the wreckage, shouting his name and sobbing as though her heart would break.

Lavinia also got out and ran down Brookmount Street to her own home, to find Robin. She was in shock, white and shaking but insisted that the two of them go back to the scene of the explosion. By now the street was a hive of activity as the police, army, fire brigade and ambulance service moved into action. They found Lavinia's friend quite quickly and were relieved to hear that her boyfriend was safe. Then they stood with many others for a moment or two to watch as the rescue work went on and what they witnessed that night left them shaken and sickened. There seemed to be blood everywhere; dead bodies were being removed from the piles of rubble as stricken relatives stood in stunned silence; injured people sat waiting for ambulances with blankets wrapped round them, their eyes glazed in shock and policemen and soldiers were carrying away severed limbs in bags.

Over and over again Lavinia kept thinking, "If the taxi driver hadn't stopped to let me out first, we would have been right there when the bomb went off." As the realisation of what might have happened hit Lavinia, she started to shake again, feeling weak and sick but so grateful to Almighty God for sparing her life. The uncontrollable shaking continued all night, and for a long time afterwards, she refused to walk past public houses but would cross the road again and again to avoid them.

This was, of course, no isolated incident and all four of them lived with danger never far away and all four could testify, like Lavinia, of near misses and miraculous escapes in city streets where terrorists fought their war against law and order.

Those days on the road were memorable not just for the evidence of God's blessing and power in their ministry but also for the sweet fellowship they enjoyed with other groups. They were very friendly with a group called "Rose of Sharon" and often went on outings together.

One fine afternoon they made their way to Newtownards and climbed up Scrabo Tower, a stone tower that overlooked the town and the surrounding countryside. As they sat on the grass at the top, looking down on the breathtaking view stretched out below them, one of the group began to sing. The young clear voice rang out in the stillness of the summer afternoon, and one by one the rest of the group joined in, interweaving beautiful harmonies around the simple melody of the gospel song. As they finished singing, a man who had also been enjoying the wonderful view came over to speak to them.

"Oh what lovely singing," he said. "I'm the Pastor of a church in America. Would you like to come and sing in my church?"

There was no way that these young people who lived on a shoestring, who refused even to take petrol money from the places where they sang, could have afforded to go to America but the request instilled in Lavinia's heart a dream to sing the praises of God in America. It's a dream that remains, that has never been realised - yet!

One of their most exciting adventures was a camping weekend in Portstewart, a holiday resort on the north coast. It wouldn't have been Lavinia's first choice of a holiday - she didn't enjoy tenting - but it was cheap, so she agreed to go. The weather was fairly typical for Portstewart - wild and windy - and the torch Lavinia had brought attracted all the insects for miles around but the three young women were not going to let their standards slip just because they were in a tent! They all got out their rollers and proceeded to set their hair, though with

The Persuaders, on the road.

great difficulty as they had forgotten to bring a mirror. The men laughed at the strange ways of the female species and the women had to laugh as well when their lovely hairstyles were completely ruined the next morning the moment they put their heads round the tent flap.

The ruined hairstyles were soon forgotten as they made their way to a quiet dip in the sand dunes behind the beautiful strand at Portstewart. There are few places so quiet as a dip in sand hills - the world seems to recede, leaving one conscious only of sand and grasses and sky. Only very faintly in the distance can be heard the rhythmic splash of the waves on the shore and the cry of a seagull. It is a perfect place in which to worship, a place where it is easy to focus on the Lord, undistracted by the world.

The seven of them settled quietly in a circle on the soft sand, the men began to strum the guitars and soon songs of praise rose up into the sky from that little hollow. They worshipped and prayed and had communion together. As they passed bread and wine to each other, remembering the One who was the focus and inspiration of their song, they knew that they were making a very special memory.

Chapter 18 ❧

IF YOU WILL GIVE ME A SON

1974 marked the end of an era for Lavinia. Lucy had been ill off and on for years with a throat problem and no explanation had ever been found so it was always put down to "her nerves". Eventually her doctor thought it might be her thyroid and after the usual examinations and tests, it was decided that it should be removed. When the operation was finished, the surgeon called Lavinia and Robin in to speak to them. They were very shocked to hear him say that Lucy had cancer of the throat and that in his estimation she had only four months to live.

The months that followed were difficult. Suddenly the parent had become the child and Lavinia had to adjust to having her mother totally dependent on her. Lucy was so terrified of hospitals that she cried to get home soon after the operation so the doctors agreed that she could receive the rest of her treatment as an outpatient. A course of chemotherapy was arranged and Lavinia travelled with her every day to the Royal Victoria Hospital for the appointments. Although Lavinia and Robin were aware of the nature of Lucy's illness, it was decided not to tell Lucy herself because of her nervous disposition and her fear of being admitted to hospital.

They decided that she would have to live with them so they all moved to a house in the Ballygomartin Road and Lavinia started the painful process of learning how to nurse her mother. She was still very young and had never nursed anyone before so it was doubly difficult to cope with someone who was dying. As Lucy grew weaker, Lavinia had to cope with feeding and attending to all her needs. Despite being so ill, Lucy still wanted to look good and insisted that Lavinia keep up her morning beauty routine of smoothing Nivea cream into her face. Because the cancer was in her throat, she had great difficulty swallowing and her food had to be specially prepared. The situation was further complicated by a strike called by the Ulster Volunteer Force which necessitated the hospital being put on an emergency supply. This meant that the hospital could not admit Lucy and was even unable to send a nurse out to help Lavinia until the last week of her illness. Lavinia's friend Maisie, who had shared so many good times with her now undertook to share the bad times and was a great support to her, helping with the nursing and encouraging her in her distress. In the evenings, Robin used to sit with Lucy and read the Bible to her and sometimes they would sing to her. These simple songs of God's love and faithfulness brought comfort to Lucy and helped to calm the awful fear she was experiencing.

The nurse eventually managed to get a bed for Lucy in Beaconsfield Hospital and she was admitted that afternoon. The nurse who was looking after her said to Lavinia, "Do you know that your mother is not long for this world?"

Lavinia assured her that they had known for quite a few days. The nurse then suggested that she should go home to rest and they would ring when she died.

"What will happen Nurse? Will she know I'm not there?" asked Lavinia.

"No dear," was the reply, "we'll be giving her an injection soon to sedate her and it is very likely that she will not waken up again."

Reassured by the nurse's words and feeling very weary after the long weeks of nursing, Lavinia and Robin went home. The phone rang at 4 am with the news that Lucy had passed away a little earlier.

When the moment Lavinia had dreaded actually came, she felt more relief than sadness. Lucy's suffering was over, she would never know weakness or pain again, she was with Jesus. For despite a faith that was weak at times, Lavinia was sure that Lucy had died trusting in Jesus and just for a moment she smiled as she thought of the spirited mother she had known and loved, who had joined with such gusto the noise and clamour of the mob, joining in the worship of heaven with equal passion and excitement.

Much of Lavinia's grieving had already been done in the months of Lucy's illness and she found that, instead of needing people to comfort her, she herself was able to comfort others. She knew God's strength and peace in great measure and had come to understand a truth that would comfort her all of her life.

"That is what death is like - peace."

Lucy's brother, Billy, came to the wake the next day and she and Robin were able to sing Gospel songs to him.

The one thing Lavinia did find hard to deal with in the days following Lucy's death was hearing people say that her mother was dead. For that reason she decided not to go to Lucy's funeral but said her own private goodbye later when she brought a wreath to the cemetery. As she stood beside the flower covered grave, she said a prayer of thanks for Lucy, who had done her best, often in extremely difficult circumstances, to look after her and provide a home for her and she said goodbye, not just to her mother, but also to her childhood.

A period of mourning followed and it was during this period that the Pastor's wife, Grace Forsythe, came alongside her, becoming almost a substitute mother to Lavinia. She was a strong, capable lady who had spent some years on the mission field and had a wealth of wisdom and experience to share. She taught Lavinia practical things, like how to bake and she passed on to her something of her own philosophy of life. She believed strongly that there was more to the Christian life than just attending meetings and encouraged Lavinia over and over again to concentrate on deepening her own personal relationship with Jesus. She had learnt how to handle the difficult times and often reminded her "adopted" daughter, "In acceptance lies peace."

She and her husband believed passionately in the value of the ministry of the Persuaders and showed their love for them by inviting them to share their Christmas Day celebrations. So began a tradition that has continued to the present day, for Lavinia and Robin still spend Christmas Day with Grace.

In the months that followed, Lucy's death triggered a loneliness in Lavinia, a sense of no longer belonging to a family. The trauma of Catreen's death had eased and for the first time in five years, Lavinia began to think again about having a baby. One Saturday morning in 1975 Lavinia was in the church, taking her turn to do the cleaning. She hoovered the carpet, then fetched the polish and began to polish the pews. She got half way up on the right hand side when she suddenly put down the polish and duster, obeying an inner compulsion that she didn't fully understand but recognised as a call to prayer. She walked to the communion table at the front and then felt compelled to kneel at the chair on the right. She had no idea what she was to pray for but simply put her head in her hands and began to worship. All at once she found herself praying Hannah's prayer from 1 Samuel chapter 1.

"O Lord, if you will give me a son, then I will give him to the Lord for all the days of his life."

She continued in prayer for a long time then felt she was being lifted up from where she knelt. The duster and the polish were left behind as Lavinia made her way home to think through what had happened. The next day when she saw Maisie she told her,

"I'm going to have a baby!"

Maisie's question was a practical one.

"Have you had a test then?"

"No," replied Lavinia but nothing would shake her strong belief that she was to have a child. When, some weeks later, the pregnancy was confirmed, the two friends rejoiced together, for Maisie was also expecting a baby.

Strangely enough, Lavinia didn't worry at all about the baby during the long months of pregnancy. She felt that she had been given God's promise and such was the simplicity and strength of her faith that she just took God at His word. She was even convinced that she would have a son.

The two "ladies-in-waiting" in the group continued to sing. They bought new outfits that allowed plenty of room for their expanding waistlines and two tall stools so that they could sit to sing when necessary. Somehow it seemed to be very important to keep on singing and Lavinia continued to go out with the group until a few days before the birth. Even their Pastor remarked on it.

"Those two children will be musical," he said, "you haven't stopped singing the whole time."

The baby grew so big that the doctors decided to induce labour three weeks before the due date. Lavinia set off for the Royal Maternity Hospital yet again, this time in a state of high excitement. There was an atmosphere of celebration in the ward even before delivery. The doctors and other patients felt the bump and tried to guess what weight the baby would be. Even when the twenty hour labour began, the pain and discomfort couldn't destroy Lavinia's excitement and anticipation. This child was alive and no amount of pain would reduce her joy. One of the nurses was intrigued by her attitude and kept telling Lavinia, "You're a strange woman. You're marvellous."

At long last, the baby was delivered - a boy called Robin after his father, a big baby 9lb 1oz. Lavinia caught a glimpse, as she had before of black hair and called out, "Is he alright? Is he breathing?"

At that moment she heard a sound that was sweeter than music to her ears - her healthy little baby's first cry - and all at once there exploded in her heart such an upsurge of love and joy that it could hardly be contained. Lavinia cried and laughed and hugged her little son close to her.

Robin meanwhile, had been impatiently waiting in the corridor outside, pacing up and down feeling rather helpless.

"You have a son," the nurse told him "They're both well. Come in and see them."

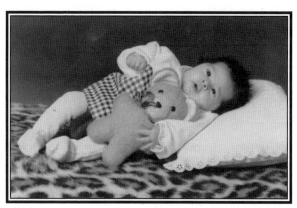

Robin at three weeks old.

He hurried to Lavinia's bedside and together they gazed at their little son, marvelling at his perfection and his resemblance to Robin. They talked excitedly about how big he was, stroked his velvety cheek with tender fingers and covered his fine black hair with kisses. Together they thanked God for this wonderful gift of a new life entrusted to their care.

Having once seen him, Lavinia could hardly bear to let him out of her sight. She refused to leave him at meal times to go to the dining room and the nurses had to keep bringing her meals to the ward. She spend hour after hour, watching him sleep, listening to his little snuffles, smiling fondly as he stretched, screwed up his face and began to wail indignantly for his feed. She prayed over him and sang to him and told him the story of the day she asked God for him. Her heart was filled with wonder as she realised that lying in the tiny hospital cot was the fulfilment of God's promise to her and she vowed that she would keep her part of the promise and "give him to the Lord all the days of his life."

She didn't know what the future held for this child but she was convinced that God had a special plan for his life. His destiny would be powerful.

❧

Chapter 19 🐦

WOMEN TALKING

"Hi Maisie, it's only me."

"I thought it might be you when I heard the phone. Hi Lavinia, how's that wee son of yours? Still sleeping all the time?"

"He's sleeping so much that I have to waken him up to feed him."

"Well aren't you the lucky one. Janine still wakes up twice a night."

"You must be exhausted, you poor soul. Now tell me, what did the Lord say to you this morning?"

"Ah Lavinia, it was just as if He was speaking right to me. He gave me that lovely verse about running and not being weary and having our strength renewed. Somehow I didn't feel so tired afterwards."

"Isn't God good, Maisie. He knows just what we need. I was having such a good time with the Lord while young Robin was sleeping that I nearly forgot to get the cleaning and the ironing done!"

Conversations like this could be heard most mornings. Lavinia and Maisie had formed such a close bond in grief, in fellowship and service and now in the joy of motherhood that they just had to be in the closest possible contact. The phone line was kept busy, so much so that their husbands threatened to have the phones taken out.

The Perusaders were soon back on the road again, this time with two new members, Robin and Janine. It used to be difficult enough to fit guitars, amplifiers, microphones and stands into the car but it became almost impossible when babies, bottles, nappies and buggies all had to fit in too. The last question asked before setting off was always, "Have you got the golliwog?" The golliwog was a vital piece of equipment, as Robin wouldn't sleep without it.

Despite the difficulties and the weariness, there was no question of them refusing engagements. The only question they discussed was whether or not it would be safe to bring the babies along. The two Mums were determined to bring both babies with them whenever possible. Lavinia took very seriously the promise she had made to God that if He gave her a son "from henceforth he will not depart from Your house." So Robin was brought to church at every opportunity, slept happily through their twice weekly practices and prayer times and travelled all over Northern Ireland to their engagements.

The potential danger to the babies wasn't necessarily associated only with far-flung places like the murder triangle. Sometimes it was just as dangerous in their own church. This was brought home very forcibly to Maisie and Lavinia one evening when Robin was four months old. They had been booked to sing at home that evening, in their own church coffee bar. The babies were there as usual - they never even thought of leaving them behind. The church was next door to a pub called the Long Bar and while the coffee bar was taking place, a gunman walked into the pub and in cold blood shot a man who was sitting there. Word of the shooting went round the streets like wildfire and within minutes an angry crowd had gathered, police cars and ambulances had shrieked to a halt outside, and the paramilitaries had swung into action, faces masked with balaclavas, guns at the ready, taking cars by force to set up barricades.

Those who ran the coffee bar were now faced with the enormous responsibility of making sure that the crowd of teenagers who had gathered for the coffee bar got home safely. One of the leaders, Jimmy Magee, risked his own life by going to the paramilitaries and begging them to let the teenagers go. He got a reluctant agreement from them and they all began leaving the coffee bar.

Robin and Sammy ran to get the car while Maisie and Lavinia took the babies into their arms and made a run for it too, praying all the time for their babies' safety. Suddenly the paramilitaries started to shoot again and for an awful moment, the women thought they were going to be caught in the crossfire. The flung themselves into the car and sped away quickly, their hearts pounding every time they heard a shot. Prayers of thanksgiving were offered up when they eventually arrived home safely.

The Persuaders sang because they had to. God had written songs on their hearts that had to be sung. For Lavinia, singing was when she was happiest, when she was most alive, when she felt closest to God. Worship and expressing that worship in song was like a deepseated passion with her. She was delighted to discover a poem written by Sylvia Sandys, called "The Divine Compulsion" for she recognised in it an attitude to ministry that was very close to her own.

The Divine Compulsion

I cannot stay ...
For I caught a glimpse of his tear-stained face,
And the longing in his eyes
So I must travel at lightning pace
Before my brother dies.

I must not stay ...
For he shared with me the ache in his heart
Over this needy land.
And he bade me go and play my part
In work which he has planned

I dare not stay ...
For the mighty force of his love he revealed
Over just one lost sheep,
And he showed me a whitened harvest field
With nobody there to reap.

No one in the group had any musical training and no one could read music, so their songs were all learnt from records and tapes. Their Pastor's wife Grace brought them a song book from America that turned out to have a profound influence on their music. It was a book of songs written and sung by the Gaither trio. When Lavinia first played them, she felt a strange affinity with them. She loved the honesty of the lyrics - the Gaithers were not afraid to acknowledge failure and sin and in a strong way Lavinia felt that they gave her a freedom to fail that other songs she knew didn't. She loved the wonderful melodies created by this talented group. They were the sort of melodies that touched the heart and remained in the memory. When she later heard one of their tapes, she loved the smooth sound produced by the blending of the three voices and she and the others in the group listened carefully to the tape so that they could try and reproduce the same harmonies and achieve the same sound. Songs like "He touched Me" released something within Lavinia that to this day has never left her.

Despite their lack of training, people were blessed by their music and often when they sang in meetings, there were those who trusted the Lord. The term "anointed" was used many times to describe their ministry. One much requested song was used in a powerful way to reach into hearts. It was called "Standing Room Only" and spoke of a coming Judgement Day. No matter how many times she sang it, Lavinia could never get past some of the lines without breaking down. As the listeners watched the tears roll down her cheeks, they too came to realise the serious implications of lines like these,

"I heard a pitiful cry for mercy
And I realised that it was for me
I didn't know Him yesterday
And He knew me not today".

The group had very little money and when they needed new, bigger speakers for the PA system, the men decided to build them. The project took up all their spare time and was the subject of much discussion - how big should they be? - where would they buy the special cloth for the front? Eventually they were completed and tested and ready to go on the road with them.

As a result of all the excitement surrounding the new speakers, they were very much in Lavinia's mind one day when she took a booking for the group to sing at a big tent meeting in the country.

In the course of the conversation, Lavinia was asked, "Do you have any speakers?" to which she very proudly answered, "Oh yes, we have two speakers."

"Well, we only need one," was the reply.

"Oh no," insisted Lavinia, "we always use two."

"OK then, that will be fine with us," said the man, the booking was made and Lavinia thought no more of the conversation.

When they arrived at the tent they unpacked all their equipment, including their two new speakers and Lavinia went to ask the person who had booked them how many songs they were to do.

"Do as many as you like," he said, "now who are your two speakers?"

Suddenly the conversation on the phone came flooding back to Lavinia and she stood dumbstruck as she realised that they had to take the whole meeting. She found Maisie and told her the whole story.

"I don't know how to tell these men that one of them is preaching," she finished, hoping for some encouragement from Maisie.

"You needn't bother - they'll both die!" was Maisie's frank opinion on the situation. Lavinia went to Sammy and tentatively asked,

"Will you give a wee word?"

But she got no encouragement from Sammy either.

"Are ye daft?" he said, his look of utter horror giving her the answer.

She then went to Robin with the same question but he would only agree to give his testimony to fill in the time. Now feeling desperate, she hurried back to Maisie.

"What are we going to do?" she cried.

They knew they couldn't sing for the two hours and they also knew that some time during the meeting, the babies would need to be fed and changed. It all seemed rather impossible but suddenly Maisie had a moment of inspiration. "Why don't we just talk about the Lord to each other?"

The four of them quickly made their plans, prayed that the Lord would bring blessing out of the mistake that had been made and went ahead with the meeting. They put two chairs at the back of the platform and brought the babies in their buggies up with them.

By the time the group had sung four songs, Janine and Robin were beginning to stir to they brought the chairs forward. The women sat down and began to feed the babies at the front of the platform.

"Well, tell me Maisie, what did the Lord say to you today?" asked Lavinia.

They talked about the Lord just the way they were used doing every morning on the phone, until the bottles were finished. They winded the babies, put them back in their buggies and rocked them while the group sang another song. Then the men gave their testimonies while Lavinia and Maisie changed their babies' nappies, down behind the back of the platform.

The people in the meeting loved it and thought that it was all part of a carefully planned programme. They realised that this was something the Lord could use and bless so "women talking" became a regular feature at their engagements.

The babies grew and became a little less predictable, a little less co-operative and a little less sleepy. The Mums used to give them apples to eat to keep them busy and quiet but Robin's apple became a source of great embarrassment to them one evening. They were sitting at the front listening to Ben Forde singing. When he finished his song, Robin who was about ten months old at this time, lifted up his arm and threw his apple at

The Persuaders, on the road with the babies, Janine and Robin Jr.

Ben. The singer picked it up and gave it back to him. From then on he used to tease the group by saying that he had got used to having missiles thrown at him in the course of his duty as a policeman but he didn't really expect to have apples chucked at him in a Christian meeting!

Chapter 20 🐦

SURRENDER

Lavinia put her hand over her mouth in an attempt to stifle a yawn and opened her eyes wide to try and stay awake. She thought that the others in the group hadn't noticed but Robin looked over and asked, "Whatever is the matter with you this evening, you haven't stopped yawning all night."

"I don't know what's the matter with me these days," replied Lavinia. "I feel tired all the time and sometimes I feel as sick as a dog."

"Maybe you haven't got over that flu you had a few weeks ago," suggested Maisie. "It can take a lot of you."

"That could be the reason," agreed Lavinia, "if I don't get better in a day or two, I'll see what the doctor says."

What the doctor said when she eventually went to see him came as a complete surprise to Lavinia. She was pregnant again. Robin and she had agreed that although they wanted six children, they would have to be carefully planned to fit in with their extremely busy life on the road. They thought it would be sensible to wait for three years after Robin's birth before having another child but God had other plans, plans that were perfect in their timing and so Lavinia found herself pregnant again when Robin was about sixteen months old.

After the initial shock, Lavinia was delighted with the news and, secure in the knowledge that her previous pregnancy had gone smoothly, actually enjoyed this pregnancy very much. Robin on the other hand, did not enjoy it at all, because he unfortunately suffered many of the strange symptoms of pregnancy instead of Lavinia. The most distressing of these was a sore back which eventually became so annoying he went to consult the doctor. He didn't get a lot of help or sympathy from the doctor, who could still remember the problems Robin had experienced throughout the previous pregnancy. He simply sent him home again with the encouraging words,

"Never mind, Mr Abrol, your back will get better just as soon as your wife has had this baby!"

The group kept to their busy schedule of singing engagements during the pregnancy and began to be well known throughout the Province. They were often asked if they had made a record and received so much encouragement to do so that they began to make enquiries about the possibility. Two record companies, Pilgrim and Shalom Recordings were prepared to take them on and they decided to accept Shalom's offer as they were based in Northern Ireland.

So began a period of great excitement - choosing the pieces they would record; rehearsing them rigorously so that they would be perfect; working out what to put on the cover; imagining what it would feel like to walk into a shop and see their record on sale.

They spent three memorable days in Eric Black's recording studio near Portadown, laying down the guitar track first, then the melody line, then filling in the harmonies. They were busy, tiring days, playing and singing for hours, sometimes going over and over a particular section, trying to achieve the sound they wanted. When they had recorded these parts, session musicians were brought into lay down other tracks and then Eric and his engineers did the final mix.

A few weeks later, the big moment arrived - they were able to hold in their hands a copy of their own record with the

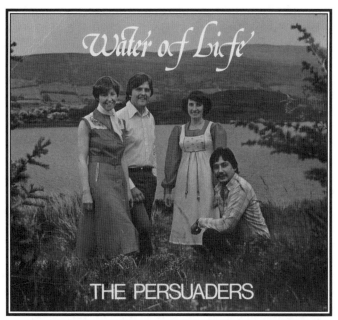

The record cover. Robin wrote most of the songs on this album.

photograph of the four Persuaders on the front cover. It was the strangest experience, hearing their voices on a record. Like most recordings, there were times when they thought,

"Oh no, do we really sound like that?" and other times when they turned to each other and said, "Now that doesn't sound too bad. The harmonies have come out really well there." It wasn't a record that was destined to hit the big time but those who loved their music were keen to buy it and many were blessed through listening to the songs they had recorded. Altogether it was a great experience, another special memory to take out and cherish in later years.

Lavinia actually saw and heard the record for the first time in hospital. She was now eight months pregnant and it had been decided to induce labour early because of the size of the baby and Lavinia's history of stillbirth. A date was carefully chosen so that an anaesthetist would be on hand should a Caesarean Section be necessary and everyone settled down to wait for the appointed day - except the baby! The night after they chose the date, Lavinia began to feel contractions. She was taken to the delivery ward and warned that it would probably be a long labour. So once again she settled down to wait and once again the baby had other ideas! A doctor was called and Robin was sent for but this baby wasn't going to wait for anyone and was born before either of them arrived. The labour had lasted just four hours from beginning to end.

And so Paul Johnston Abrol was born, another dark haired, brown eyed little baby. Twenty one years later, in a story to commemorate his coming of age, Lavinia would express how she felt at that moment:-

"They put you in my arms and you were wide awake, staring at me. I cried as I said 'hello'. You kept looking at me. It was as if we had always known each other, we were the same somehow. That's the way it was always to be."

Robin arrived fifteen minutes later and couldn't believe that Paul had been born so quickly. The doctor, who didn't arrive until Lavinia was back in the post natal ward, was equally amazed and kept asking her if she was alright. Lavinia felt wonderful and was just so excited about her new baby boy. She introduced him to the world from the windows of the ward, telling him that soon he would be out there, seeing it all, and little Paul's wide-awake gaze seemed to say back to her, "Hurry up Mum, I can't wait. Show it all to me."

Lavinia had just three weeks to try and get the new baby into some sort of routine before going back on the road with the group. She didn't think there would be much of a problem as Robin had been such a good sleeper and she assumed Paul would be the same. Paul, as usual, had other ideas! It was as though he had decided that sleeping was a waste of time and did as little of it as possible. He didn't cry much, he just stayed awake a lot, smiling and cooing at anyone who looked at him.

When Paul was a few weeks old, Robin, who was two at this time began teething again and Lavinia was up with both children at night, exhausted and beginning to wonder if she would ever again be able to sleep through the night. But even in the midst of exhaustion, God spoke to her in a significant way in the middle of one of those broken nights.

She had just fed Paul and put him down in his cot in his own little nursery when she heard Robin crying so she went to try and settle him. His teeth were sore and he wouldn't lie down so she lifted him out of the cot and let him walk around for a while to tire him out. Eventually he began falling over because he was so tired but every time she tried to put him back in the cot to sleep, he started crying and pulling himself up again. For the next three hours he struggled against sleep, despite needing it so much until at half past three in the morning, he finally gave in. Lavinia leaned over the cot, watching him sleeping peacefully, the signs of his tremendous struggle still evident in his little red cheeks and the tears on his eyelids. She sensed God speak into her heart as she stood there and began to cry over all the struggles in her own life - struggles to do things her own way, struggles caused by her wilfulness. She recognised that just like little Robin, every time she struggled against God, she fell over. Despite having been a Christian for fourteen years, she knew that she had never fully made Him Lord of all. As she fell on her knees, surrendering her will to His, she sensed that God was doing a work deep inside, a work of refreshing and healing. His peace enveloped her and she got up, found pen and paper and wrote a letter to the Lord.

"To my Friend,

I love you because You first loved me. There is no way I will ever forget Your undying love towards me. Why did You choose me? I had nothing to offer only a broken and confused life. Yet You touched my life and are still shaping and making me, conforming me to Your image. What a job You took on. I'm glad that You are patient or You'd have given up long ago. Please don't give up on me. If You'd not been with me all these years, I don't know where my life would have taken me. I can't live without You now, I've known You too long. When sorrow and despair take hold of my life You are my joy and You have given me a song in my heart that I want to sing to the 'Great Musician' forever.

You have used strange paths in my life. Many of my lessons have been learnt through tears but I know that those lessons were for my benefit. There is a love bond between us that will never be broken, sealed by Your precious blood and yes, Your blood has been special to me. May I become special to You as we continue our friendship. You are the measure of all that I ever want to be so please stay with me and keeping working on my life and may my only desire be to do Your will. Keep me surrendered to You Lord, for only in complete surrender can I be used in Your plan.

Please don't ever give up on me, I need You more and more as day passes day. I hope that You need me even just a little.

Your loving servant,
Lavinia Abrol

It was half past four in the morning before Lavinia finished. She hadn't been to bed all night and it was time for Paul's next feed but somehow she didn't feel tired. She made her way up to Paul's room, picked him up and watched the dawn break as she fed him. She sensed that something significant had just happened and knew that in the years to come she would prove what her Pastor had often said - that time spent with God was never wasted. Prayer, she would come realise, is like a bank. Lodgements are made during good times so that when bad times arrive, there are sufficient riches in the storehouse for withdrawals to be made with interest.

And the angel who watched smiled with delight that one of earth's sinful creatures should know the joy that all of Heaven's angels knew so well, the joy of bowing the knee in surrender before the God of the universe and crying out in worship, "Holy! Holy! Holy!"

Chapter 21 ❧

PLEASE DON'T DO THIS TO ME

Paul was in many respects a wonderful baby and Lavinia knew hours of happiness as she carried him around the house, singing and talking to him while she did her chores. Two year old Robin wasn't jealous at all but seemed fascinated by this tiny baby. He was happy to help his Mum by fetching and carrying for her and constantly asked to hold Paul.

The group began singing again very quickly. In fact, Paul was just one week old when they sang at his dedication service. His fond Mum always maintained that he recognised the sound of the Persuaders because as they began to sing, he turned his head towards the platform. As they had done at Robin's dedication, they sang one of the Gaither pieces which included the following words:-

> *"How sweet to hold a new born baby,*
> *And feel the pride and joy he brings,*
> *But sweeter still, the calm assurance,*
> *This child can face uncertain days,*
> *Because He lives."*

A visiting preacher from America dedicated Paul to the Lord and prayed that God would use him mightily and that many would be touched by his life. Like Mary of old, Lavinia hid these words in her heart. So strong was her belief that her boys would come to know the Lord, that she never prayed for them to become Christians but rather that they would be called into full time Christian work.

There was really just one problem with Paul - it became obvious as time went on that he was a poor sleeper and as the weeks of sleepless nights turned into months, Lavinia got more and more desperate for a good night's sleep. She tried everything that everyone suggested - she gave him extra food at night, made sure he was warm enough, got medicine from the chemist - but nothing worked. He simply dozed for an hour or two and then was wide-awake and smiling at the world again.

She even tried moving him out of the nursery and placing his cot beside her bed, hoping that being able to see her when he woke would help the problem. The baby liked to hold her fingers so she tried sleeping with one arm stretched through the bars of his cot so that he could grasp her finger at any time. This only kept him happy for a few hours then he would wonder why his lazy Mum wanted to be in bed when she could be talking or singing to him.

At the end of two years, an exhausted Robin and Lavinia finally decided that Paul just didn't need much sleep. A nursery gate was placed at the top of the stairs and Paul was allowed to get up and play when he felt like it. It was definitely not an ideal arrangement but at least Robin and Lavinia were able to sleep a little while Paul played quite happily with his toys.

By the time Paul was three years old, it was obvious that he had a problem with his right foot. They noticed that when he walked it didn't look quite right. His right foot seemed to be turned in and sometimes he even tripped over it, so Lavinia made an appointment with the doctor, who sent them to the hospital for an X-ray. After X-raying his feet, legs, pelvis and spine the doctor concluded that, as nothing appeared to be wrong, Paul must have developed a habit of walking wrongly.

Paul, who never wanted to sleep, aged six months.

"Can anything be done to make it better?" asked Lavinia.

"Oh yes," replied the doctor, "it could be corrected by wearing surgical boots. I'll ask the nurse to bring in some boots his size."

Lavinia had never seen surgical boots before and she was horrified when the nurse brought them in. They were held together by an iron bar and her stomach lurched at the thought of her active little boy having to wear something so ugly and restrictive.

The doctor noticed her dismay.

"Mrs Abrol, you mustn't worry. This treatment is always most successful. Paul will be walking normally in no time at all," he said.

Lavinia looked at the doctor and begged, "Please don't do this to me."

When the doctor enquired why, she tried to explain, "Doctor, this child hasn't slept a full night since he was born. If I put him into these, he'll never sleep at all."

"Well I'm sorry" was his reply, "but it is the only way to correct the problem."

So the surgical boots were brought home and put on Paul's feet at bedtime. Paul had his own way of dealing with them and by the time he reached his bedroom, he could do bunny hops in them. With a heavy heart, Lavinia put him into bed and prepared herself for the worst night yet.

Some time later she woke up, feeling as if she had been drugged. She looked at the clock and gasped in astonishment. It was seven o'clock! She shook Robin, "Waken up! There's something wrong with Paul. It's seven o'clock!"

Robin stirred sleepily and grunted unintelligibly, trying to understand how the time and something being wrong with Paul were connected. Lavinia pushed back the covers and rushed out of the room shouting, "There must be something wrong. He hasn't wakened all night!"

Convinced now that he had died in his sleep, she ran to Paul's room to find him just waking up. He gave her a big smile and her legs turned to jelly with relief. Paul had slept through the night for the first time in three years. Somehow the iron bar that held his surgical boots in place must have sufficiently immobilised him to prevent him getting out of bed. Lavinia remembered the words she had spoken to the doctor, "Please don't do this to me," and realised the very thing she thought would make things unbearable actually made things better.

She also realised that God was teaching her a lesson for life in what had happened and in later years would look back and reflect that the same principle applied in her walk with the Lord.

"There have been times in my life when I have said to God 'Please don't do this to me.' Yet always the sorrows have made me into something better, stronger and wiser. God knows what He is doing."

God also knew that one of the most effective ways to get Lavinia's attention was through her children, especially through the things they said. Paul developed an endearing little habit of lifting his arms to Lavinia and saying, "Mummy, give me you."

Even though he was just a tiny little boy, Lavinia felt that he had somehow sensed that when she picked him up for a cuddle, she was actually giving to him something of herself, that there was more than just the physical hug involved. She came to realise that she could use the child's quaint little saying to express her own desire to be loved by the God of Heaven and often in her own quiet times, would lift up her arms in worship, praying, "Father, give me You."

And God Almighty would give of Himself, enfolding her in His presence, engulfing her with His peace and joy.

When the boys were a little older, Robin dropped into her life God's own challenge to her heart, through one of his colourful expressions. Quite often, on a warm summer day during the holidays, Lavinia would get everyone ready early, pack the car with toys and food and her guitar and Bible and head to the nearest beach for her quiet time. The boys would play contentedly on the usually deserted beach, leaving Lavinia free to sing and read and pray.

On the way to the beach for one of their picnics, they passed a horse grazing in a field, a sandy-coloured horse. Robin looked at it for a moment, then leaned across to Lavinia and said, "Mammy, look at that horse - it's like gold that's forgotten to shine."

The phrase he used kept coming back to Lavinia for the rest of the day. She thought of her own life and how easily she forgot to shine. She was sure that she had read something similar in the Bible and hunted until she found a verse in Lamentations chapter 4, which said, "How the gold has lost its lustre, the fine gold become dull!"

From then on, when she was asked to speak at meetings, she often used that verse to bring God's challenge to other Christians to keep shining for Him.

❧

Chapter 22 ❧

COUNTRY LIVING

Phut, phut, phut, phut!

Lavinia awoke with a start and sat bolt upright in bed. She checked the clock. It was one o'clock in the morning. Living on the Ballygomartin Road had accustomed her to the sound of gunfire but this sounded really close. She jumped out of bed to see if she could find out what was wrong and was just about to pull the curtain aside to peep out when Robin shouted, "Don't look! Don't open the curtains! Someone might see you!"

There was another burst of machine gun fire and then silence. Robin pulled on some clothes, went downstairs, opened the door and stepped outside, checking carefully all the time that it was safe enough to investigate. There on the road, parked at a crazy angle right outside their house, was a car with bullet holes in the windscreen. One of the men inside was clutching his stomach where the blood was oozing out fast. His face was contorted with pain and anger. Another lay slumped in his seat, ominously silent and still. Robin learned what had happened from one his neighbours in the crowd that had gathered. The three men in the car had opened fire on some soldiers further down the road. As they raced away from the scene, they were met by another army patrol who opened fire, killing one man instantly and injuring another. The third occupant of the car managed to escape.

As the ambulance and police began to arrive, Robin went back into the house to tell Lavinia what was happening. He found her in the boys' bedroom, sitting on one of the beds with tears streaming down her face.

"What's the matter? Are the boys alright?" he asked.

"I was so scared to come into the nursery," Lavinia replied, her voice still shaking with emotion. "I was so sure the bullets had come into the house. I was convinced that at least one of them would be dead. I thought I would hear them crying - that the machine gun fire would have wakened them up. I was so frightened when I didn't hear anything."

The boys continued to sleep, unaware of all the drama around them.

She continued to cry as Robin explained to her what had happened outside. She was appalled to think that a man had been killed right outside her front door.

"Oh Robin, we need to get away from here. This is no place to bring up two wee children."

The street was in an uproar for the rest of the night and as Lavinia listened to the sounds of army jeeps and police cars and ambulances; as the dead and injured men were taken away; as the police began taking statements from the people standing around, she became more and more convinced that to move house would be best for all of them. The past few months had been particularly difficult, for many reasons and it seemed as though God was allowing the soil around their roots to be loosened.

One of the more painful situations which Lavinia had faced, had been a pregnancy that ended in miscarriage. She had been very sick throughout the pregnancy and at fourteen weeks felt sure that things were going wrong. The doctor tried to assure her that all would be fine but arranged a scan for her. Much to her disappointment, the scan revealed that the baby had died a couple of weeks earlier. She was admitted to hospital and suddenly it was all over. Lavinia found it very hard to believe. She hadn't considered for a moment that she might lose this baby - after all hadn't she produced two healthy sons? She had often heard others say that most women would lose one baby in their lifetime, but she didn't expect to lose two.

Although she felt the pain very keenly, it was different to the pain of losing Catreen. Not having to deliver the baby made a difference and her two little boys were a source of great comfort to her. They came to the hospital to see her, bringing hugs and kisses and a make-up box as a present for her. There were other pressures in her life which were causing her distress so in some respects the miscarriage became just another pain in lots of pain.

Sometimes God uses the pain in our lives to move us into the place where He wants us to be, where He can be close to us and minister deeply to us. This proved to be the case in His dealings with Lavinia at this time in her life. They had often talked about moving and used to drive out of Belfast into the country, looking at places where they would like to live and dreaming a little as they drove around. The shooting incident outside their house was the final straw and they began to make it known among their friends that they were serious about moving house.

The couple who had been their best man and bridesmaid, David and Norma Porter had been living in a Unitarian Church Manse at Ballee while they were ministering in the Downpatrick Baptist Church. The time had come for them to leave the house and so they asked Robin and Lavinia if they would like their names to be put down for it. There was great excitement when they were told they could move in at Easter.

After living in Belfast for most of her life, moving to a house in the heart of the country thirty miles away was such a big adventure. It felt as though they were going into the wilderness. As the red removal lorry brought their belongings up the long drive to the old manse, Lavinia wondered if she would be able to adjust to this new, very different lifestyle.

The lorry was soon emptied and the furniture put in place. Lavinia decided to take the two boys outside to explore the huge garden. Robin continued to work on inside the house but after a short time thought he heard someone shouting outside. When he went into the garden he found Lavinia and the boys caught in the brambles in the middle of a wooded area. Lavinia had quite happily led the boys into the trees but then couldn't find a clear way back out again and all three of them were soon stuck fast in the brambles. After that little adventure they decided it might be better to explore the house first!

As Lavinia walked round the big, old fashioned manse she couldn't help but think back to the little girl who used to sit in a spartan bedroom in a tiny terraced house, wishing she could be like the girls in the stories she loved to read, girls who lived in large country homes with spacious gardens. For Lavinia, walking into the Ballee manse was like walking into a palace. The rooms were light and airy with high ceilings and panelled doors. The two reception rooms at the front of the house had elegant bay windows and old fashioned fireplaces. The oak panelled study had originally been a library and still retained an atmosphere of culture and the slightly musty smell of old books. The kitchen had a pantry attached to it that was almost as big as some of the kitchens in the Shankill Road houses.

The staircase, with its thick mahogany banister, lent an air of gracious living to the hallway. One of Lavinia's favourite features was in the wall of the landing at the top of the stairs - a lovely stained glass window that reminded her of a church. She walked round the upstairs in a daze, marvelling at the fact that she now had enough bedrooms to set aside two as guest rooms. All the rooms in the house had little bells that had been used to summon the servants from the kitchen, and the stables outside had fireplaces that used to be lit to dry out the carriage when it was wet.

Lavinia could hardly take it all in. She felt like a princess in a palace and kept wondering if she would suddenly wake up to find that it had all been a dream. She experienced an instant love for the house and knew that she would feel comfortable and at home in Ballee Manse. Of course the transformation from

Our special house in the country.

a city girl didn't happen overnight and the country living took some getting used to. She found it hard to adjust to the total darkness at night, having lived all her life in streets that were never completely dark as a result of street lighting. When one of her new neighbours called to visit and happened to mention that her husband Sydney had to bring one of his cows into the house because it was sick, Lavinia who had never heard of a cowshed being called a house, thought that her neighbours were extremely good to their animals. She did wonder just how Eileen managed to cope with a cow in her kitchen!

A few weeks after moving in, Lavinia spend a most unsettled night. She kept waking up to the sound of gunfire and spent the night tossing and turning, convinced that the troubles had followed them to Ballee.

"It's worse than Belfast," she said to Robin in the morning, "it never stops. It kept going all night. If the man they were chasing isn't dead, it'll be a miracle."

Later that day when the breadman called, Lavinia mentioned to him how bad the shooting had been the night before and was somewhat taken aback when he started to laugh.

"Oh Missus, that was a barley gun," he explained. "This is God's own country. You'll not hear shooting like that in Ballee."

Gradually life settled in to a pleasant routine. Robin left for work in Belfast each morning and young Robin started attending Downpatrick Primary School, leaving Lavinia alone to look after Paul and play "lady of the manor" in her new home. And there was a constant smile on the angelic face of the one who watched as He saw her draw closer and closer to the One whom all heaven worshipped and adored.

Chapter 23 ❧

Open House

Although Lavinia and Robin had moved to Ballee for the sake of their children, to provide a safe and suitable environment in which to rear their two little boys, it soon became apparent that God had much deeper purpose for the move. It was only natural that when they left the Shankill Road, they would invite their friends and family to visit them and soon a steady flow of visitors made their way to Ballee and took up residence in the two guest rooms. When people they didn't even know began to be sent to them, they realised that God was instigating a new ministry in their lives, a ministry of hospitality, encouragement and evangelism.

Two verses from Isaiah chapter 43 were brought to Lavinia's attention over and over again, a confirmation of God's call from His Word.

"Remember not the former things, neither consider the things of old. Behold I will do a new thing; now it shall spring forth; shall you not know it? I will make a way in the wilderness and rivers in the desert."

The house was often full as friends and strangers alike gathered for a chat or a sing song and on many occasions Lavinia had no idea how she would provide meals for them all. She had never lost her simple faith in God's ability to provide, however, and took it for granted that if God sent people to her, then He would provide the food for them. The ways He chose to do this often amused her. The better she got to know the God she served, the more convinced she became that He had a wonderful sense of humour.

The open house at Ballee extended not only to people but also to animals. Kelly the poodle had been brought with them from Belfast and Tober the cat came to them from the animal shelter. Robin and Paul were delighted when two rabbits were added to the family and were even more delighted when the very suitably named Adam and Eve decided it was their duty to replenish the earth with baby rabbits!

The menagerie grew even larger when Robin and Lavinia discovered just how difficult it was to keep the grass cut. The lawn mowers they tried all broke down before they had managed to cut more than a hundred yards, so they listened with great interest when someone suggested buying goats.

"Do you really think it will work?" Robin asked Lavinia. "I can't see how a couple of goats will manage to eat all that grass."

Lavinia was much more enthusiastic. Any excuse to have more animals around was fine by her. So Talani, Patrick and Mildred moved into the gardens of Ballee Manse and very efficiently set to work on the grass. Lavinia was really pleased with this solution to the grass cutting problems until she discovered the goats' appetite wasn't limited to grass. They just as efficiently chomped their way through the washing on the line!

It was Duffy the dog, however, that convinced Lavinia about God's wonderful sense of humour. She bought groceries every week from Duffy's grocery van and listened with growing interest one day when he started to tell her the sad tale of ten pups.

"It's one of my customers down the road," he began. "Her dog had ten pups recently and she told me that they are going to do away with them tomorrow unless I can find homes for them. I don't like the idea of them being put down. Would you not take one of them, Missus?"

"What sort of dogs are they?" Lavinia asked.

"Mongrels really, but I think they'll grow up to look like Labradors. There's a wee black fellow with a white flash on his chest. What about having him?"

Lavinia was easily persuaded and agreed to take the pup. Later that night she managed to persuade Robin that a new pup would make the ideal Christmas present for the two boys. The grocer must have been a good salesman for by the end of the day he had persuaded nine other customers to rescue a pup from certain death. So Duffy came to stay and was given the name of his rescuer. Lavinia and Robin managed to hide him in the garage until Christmas morning when they presented him to the boys amid great cries of delight.

There was just one problem with Duffy - he was a thief - but it was his thieving tendencies that Lavinia believed was used of the Lord on more than one occasion to provide for the large numbers of people who ended up in her house. He once pulled a bunch of carrots out of the ground by their green tops and carried them home unbitten and unharmed. Lavinia was able to use them in a big pot of stew.

One another evening, Lavinia sat, outwardly calm and serene, trying to look as though she was enjoying every moment of the singsong to the full. Inwardly she was anything but calm - she had a crowd of people in her house and she nothing to give them for supper, not even a loaf of bread.

"Well God," she thought, "how are you going to get us out of this one?"

Suddenly her eye was caught by a movement outside. She nudged Robin, who was aware of her predicament but had no solutions to offer.

"Isn't that Duffy coming up the drive?" she whispered. "Whatever is he bringing home this time?"

Duffy the dog who went shopping for bread.

Robin looked out, then leaned forward to get a close look.
"I'm not sure but I think it's a loaf of bread!"

Sure enough, there was the little black dog, charging up the driveway, dragging a loaf of bread. Robin and Lavinia hurried outside and were amazed to see that the bread was intact, still in its wrapper despite its unconventional method of delivery!

"Isn't God good," was Lavinia's immediate reaction. "He knew we needed bread."

"But Lavinia," protested Robin, "you can't just use someone else's bread. It must belong to one of the neighbours. I'll have to take it back."

Lavinia believed with all her heart that God had simply answered her prayer but she let Robin take the loaf around the neighbouring houses, just in case the breadman might have left it on one of their windowsills. He came back with the loaf in a little while.

"No one seems to own it," he said in a puzzled voice. "I wonder where Duffy got it?"

As Lavinia made toast for her guests she could just imagine the Lord smiling down in amusement from Heaven.

Some of the other objects stolen by Duffy were not quite so useful. When a new house was being built nearby, he kept bringing home wall sockets. At least they knew who owned them and were able to give them back. They never did discover who the owner was of the single wellington boot that he laid at her feet one day with a look that seemed to say, "Now what would you do without me?"

Many of the visitors to Ballee came, not for a singsong or a chat but for a much needed rest or period of rehabilitation. They stayed as long as they needed to, some for as little as a week, others for as long as six months. They often had little but paid for their stay by doing jobs about the house. The door was always open (literally!) and the two guest-rooms ready so their visitors sometimes even came in the middle of the night and no-one knew they were there until the next morning.

They had varying needs - some simply needed to get away for a while from the fighting and rioting in Belfast to the peace and quiet of the countryside. Some had foolishly allowed themselves to become involved in paramilitary organisations, taken part in shootings or bombings and ended up paying society's price for their crimes in prison. These ex-prisoners needed to see a different way of life at work; needed to know that God loved them and longed to forgive their sin and take away their guilt; needed to hear that the way of cross was one of peace and reconciliation; needed to learn that conflicts could be solved without violence.

These were significant days for Lavinia, days when God laid down deep within her the foundation of what would later become a counselling ministry. She quickly learnt that most people who had deep-seated problems did not need advice as much as they needed someone who would listen to them with interest and compassion. It was at this time too that God began whispering words of knowledge into her heart. Her diary entries reflected both her deep desire to reach out to those who were hurting and also her apprehension at the new way God was choosing to work though her. It seemed to Lavinia that she

Lavinia, Robin, Robin and Paul outside 'The Big House'.

often "knew" things that normally she wouldn't have known and the "knowing" frightened her. Sometimes she simply knew that someone was going to call at the house but at other times the knowledge went much deeper, enabling her to minister into their lives more effectively.

October 1981: *"I'm going to be busy this weekend Lord, meals to prepare, a party, children to organise, needs to be met. Please help me not to get so caught up in the busyness of life that I miss the real life that flows beneath all the superficial show. Help me in a special way to reach out to life … the real life that hurts and cries for help …Take my hand and walk with me into the lives of others."*

"I'm frightened Lord by the feelings and the knowledge inside me these past days. Your hand upon my life is beautiful Lord but seeing people as You see them and feeling the hurts of others, I need more of You so that I can stand the pain. Does it all have to hurt so much? Is this how it is for You?"

She recognised too that if she was to be of any help to others, it was vital that she walked close to the Lord. Walking close meant doing His will and when, as so often happens in the

Christian life, her will conflicted with His, the resulting tension was difficult to resolve.

21st May 1982: *"God is still moving strongly in my life and I'm a bit frightened by it all. It would be so easy to make a mistake and ruin this relationship with God and others. I told the Lord I wanted to be his bondslave, a few weeks ago and I've realised that to become that, other things and other people have to take second place. For to be completely led by Him is making a lot of demands on me. There are things which I would prefer to cling to but He's saying 'let go' so these times have not been so easy for me."*

Often the battle resulted in tears. Lavinia used to feel that crying was such a purposeless activity, such a waste of time until God surprised her one day with a verse from Psalm 56.

"Thou tellest my wanderings, put Thou my tears into thy bottle, are they not in Thy book?"

Her diary for that evening reads.

"Father you have seen my tears, You know all the reasons for them and Your Word tells me that You've recorded them. You see and know all things. Thank you Lord for that. I am glad that you never leave us alone but You are always there".

From that time on Lavinia used the image of God keeping her tears in a bottle to bring comfort to her own heart and also to others for whom life's circumstances meant that tears were constant companions.

Her two little boys still settled down early at night and often Lavinia went to bed at eight o'clock, so that she could spend the evening in quietness, reading her Bible and praying. God often used these evenings to give her scriptures of comfort or encouragement or rebuke which she in her turn was able to pass on to meet someone else's need in the next day or two. She became the channel though which His Word flowed, bringing His grace and His love into situations of distress and difficulty. She spent nights sitting up with a girl who had terrible depression, listening to her story of despair and then applying the balm of God's love to her wounds, helping her to find hope in her darkness.

As Lavinia continued to walk with Him, God implanted deep within her two desires as an underlying support for all of her counselling ministry - the desire to see people as God saw them and the desire to see God changing them to the way He wanted them to be. A diary entry in June 1982 spoke of both desires.

"Father I want to be a light in this world for you. I want, not just to see a world, I want to see people, individuals. I want to feel their hurts as You feel them. I want to understand them as You do. Teach me Lord."

"I feel so different this year. I seem to be a different person sometimes. You're so close, Lord, Your presence so near. You make people different. Thank You for that."

Chapter 24 🖎

OLD SINS CAST LONG SHADOWS

Lavinia lay very still, her heart pounding, her mouth dry, her skin clammy. The footsteps got louder, the door creaked open and she began to moan softly. The dark shape of the man came closer, then bent menacingly over her. He had blood on his hands and she realised with mounting terror that he intended to put it on her face. She struggled to get free but in some strange way she seemed to be pinned to the bed. As she felt the blood being smeared on her face she opened her mouth to scream but no sound came. Then in one violent motion he tipped the bed.

At that moment Lavinia awoke with a start, shaking violently with fear, the tears streaming down her face and she heard once again the whispered threat of her stepfather.

"When I'm dead and buried, I'll come and haunt you! You'll never get away from me!"

Lavinia's restlessness had wakened Robin.

"What's the matter" he asked.

"I had the nightmare again," she replied in a shaking voice. "You know, he did what he said he would do - he did come back and haunt me. Every time I think of him during the day, I have the nightmare at night. Oh I wish something could be done to stop the nightmares. Sometimes I'm afraid to go to sleep at night because I know it's going to come again."

Old sins cast long shadows and Lavinia had been living in the shadow of Davey Williams' sin against her for about twenty years. She had never told anyone the story of the abuse she had suffered or the nightmares she still endured. Like many victims of abuse, she felt too ashamed and in a strange way was convinced that there was no point in sharing what she had been through because she thought no one could possibly understand. There were no counsellors to assure her that talking about her experiences would help, so for twenty long years Lavinia had relived the terrors of her childhood in a recurring nightmare.

The shadow of her suffering interfered with her ministry too for she found that she could not work with men who reminded her of her stepfather, men like Danny.

They met Danny at an open-air meeting organised by the church they now attended, Downpatrick Baptist Church. Danny was an alcoholic, a local man, who had stopped to listen to the little group as they spoke and sang about Jesus. Robin invited him home after the meeting and while he appreciated their hospitality and friendship he found it all quite strange, a different world altogether. He knew so little about the Christian way of life that the first time he heard them all singing the new popular chorus "Majesty" he walked out of the room. They couldn't understand what had offended him so deeply until they discovered that he thought that "Majesty" was a new National Anthem and Danny was a convinced republican! When assured that the "majesty" referred to was Jesus and not the British Queen, he agreed to go back and so began a long, hard fight to help Danny break the bonds of alcoholism.

Lavinia couldn't work with him but Lawrence McDowell and Crawford Bell, a surgeon in the local hospital, took Danny under their wing. It was a battle fraught with disappointments and one which eventually ended in defeat for Danny's alcohol addiction proved to be stronger than his desire to be free of it.

Seeing a man under the influence of drink affected Lavinia deeply, often resulting in this terrifying nightmare.

This was all about to change, for God's mighty power can deal even with the shadows in our lives. As well as Crawford and Gwen Bell, who became very close friends, the little church in Downpatrick was also the means God used to introduce Roseanne into Lavinia's life and it was through Roseanne that the shadow of Davey Williams was finally dispelled.

Roseanne enjoyed singing and soon after they met, she and Lavinia began to sing together. They met each Tuesday night to practise and to pray and over a number of months a deep relationship was formed, a relationship built on love and trust. Each respected the other's close walk with the Lord and each admired the other's firm commitment to serve Him.

One summer evening in 1982, when they had finished practising and praying, they began to share their testimonies. As they talked on into the night, Lavinia felt that for the first time she had found someone to whom she could entrust her story. She felt somehow that Roseanne was strong enough to take it. So, haltingly and without going into too much detail, she told her story. Roseanne was shocked for she had just assumed that Lavinia had had a sheltered upbringing, much like her own.

When Lavinia mentioned to her that she still had nightmares about her stepfather, Roseanne seemed to realise that God did not want this to happen to His child and she very quietly said, "Maybe God wants you to forget."

She laid her hands on Lavinia and prayed a very simple prayer claiming the promise from Isaiah, "By His stripes we are healed."

Next day, Lavinia wrote in her diary,

"Last night was a special night Lord, You healed me. You touched scars in my life that were deep and really hurt at times. I don't know why it happened like it did or why You chose this time but you did and I am grateful. I am free from the 'chains of sorrow'. You used Roseanne. Is that why You told me to get to know her? Was there meant to be more than singing between us? I am sure now that this also was one of the reasons. Just a few words "Maybe God wants

you to forget." Your time Lord ... Realisation and trust ... handing it all over to you ... You gave me peace and now I don't hurt anymore but am filled with contentment and an inner peace I have never experienced in my entire life."

The nightmares were never to return.

About this time, Lavinia also began to realise more fully the extent of yet another shadow in her life - the shadow cast by Uncle Billy's insistence that all contact with her father's family must be broken. As she watched her own boys grow up and saw the rich heritage passed on to them from both parents, she came to understand why she often felt incomplete, that part of her was missing. There was within her a strong awareness that another family had contributed to her character and personality, had passed on to her the need to hug people, an appreciation of the soulful song of poetry, a talent for craft work, a love of Celtic tunes and the rhythm of the bodhran. Somewhere out there was a part of herself that she didn't know and at times the longing to discover it became overwhelming. It rose up within her on those rare occasions when she visited a chapel. After one such visit, for the christening of a friend's baby, her diary records how she felt.

"I went to chapel today. Julia and Stephen invited us to their baby's christening. It did not feel strange, it did evoke some underlying feelings. Some primeval instinct rose within me and I could see that part of myself is always elusively out there, unreachable but there.

Today as I stood in the house of my father's faith, that empty part of me that is always searching, didn't feel quite as lonely. I don't really know why, perhaps it was just the knowledge that he would have been brought as a baby the same way to receive baptism, and once again the candle of hope flickered in my heart leaving me warm and secure."

Robin and Lavinia had tried to trace her father some years before but had been unsuccessful. Lavinia would have to live in that shadow for some time yet.

There was another shadow too in which Lavinia would have to live not just for a while but for all of her life. It was the shadow cast by her own sin. It is probably true to say that we all live in the shadow of our sin for even though God loves us and forgives us and even forgets our sin, we find it really difficult, if not impossible to forgive ourselves and to forget our wrongdoing. Lavinia knew the reality of this as she looked back on her own life. Over the years she had come to recognise her weakness and Satan also knew the areas of her life that were vulnerable. No matter how closely she walked with God, her intimacy with Him did not provide immunity from temptation and sin and often the sin in her life had far reaching effects. Despite tears of repentance and remorse and determination to put things right, to keep short accounts with God, her sin cast a long shadow that marred relationships, that caused wrong decisions to be made. How thankful she was God loved her despite her sin, that no matter how many times she came to Him in repentance, His hand always reached out in mercy and forgiveness always flowed from His throne. It amazed her that He never withheld His love when she let Him down but instead reached out to draw her closer to Him. She was so grateful that she served a God who delighted to pour out, in lavish abundance, sufficient grace to cover all her sin.

The shadow of Uncle Billy's role in her difficult childhood was dealt with by God, not in an instant, as Davey's had been but over a period of years. They had always kept in touch with Uncle Billy, going to visit him each Sunday even after Lucy had died. Gradually, over the years, a relationship had built up and Uncle Billy mellowed and changed as he came to appreciate the love shown to him.

When they moved to Ballee, they brought him to stay with them for a week now and again. He enjoyed going to visit the big house in the country, talking to the people who came to visit, getting to know his great-nephews, Paul and Robin. Lavinia often looked on in amazement as she watched Uncle Billy interacting with her boys and couldn't help but remember the harsh, gruff man who had made little effort to form any sort of relationship with her in her childhood.

He wasn't in very good health at this time, having suffered a stroke and a heart attack in recent years. During one of his holidays with them, he went into heart failure during the night.

They phoned an ambulance and made him as comfortable as they could. When the ambulance arrived, the paramedic didn't offer them much hope.

"I don't think he'll make it through the night."

Lavinia was really upset, not only because he was so ill but also because she knew that Uncle Billy had not yet become a Christian. So Robin agreed to go to Downpatrick Hospital with the express purpose of challenging Uncle Billy about salvation.

"Billy," said Robin, "would you not trust the Lord?"

Despite being weak and tired and in pain, Billy managed to whisper "Yes."

Lavinia and Robin were overjoyed.

"Uncle Billy has got saved," the diary reads. *"Thank you Father. It's like a miracle".*

As Lavinia rejoiced over Uncle Billy's conversion, she was reminded of her own conversion. Time and time again in the days that followed she was caught up in the wonder of it all. She understood so much better now what had happened the night she gave her life to the Lord and the amazing miracle of salvation just took her breath away. As she looked back on the years that had followed, she could see how her relationship with Jesus had matured into 'chats' with the Lord and in one of them she asked,

"Do you remember the day I first found You ... Angel choirs rejoiced and sang as we walked hand in hand. Your arms embraced me and as I looked into Your eyes I saw Your love for me. Many years have passed since that night. Our relationship has grown. I love You more now. I love the sound of Your voice. I have come to recognise it so well now. We'll walk more roads together You and I. We'll laugh and cry and sing and one day I will be Your bride."

To the amazement of Lavinia and Robin and the doctors in the hospital, Uncle Billy pulled back from the brink of death and began to recover. He shared his sister Lucy's awe of and respect for the medical profession, so was amazed to hear Crawford, the consultant, address him as "Billy".

He did not however, have the same respect for hospital technology. On a previous visit to another hospital, he showed scant respect for the complex monitoring required for cardiac patients. As he began to regain his independence he decided one day to visit the bathroom without calling a nurse to assist him.

"I'll just slip out and they'll never hear me," he thought as he pulled the monitors off his chest. What a surprise he got when he was suddenly surrounded by three or four nurses before he had barely taken a single step! They, of course, were convinced that something had gone terribly wrong and had rushed into the ward, ready to alert the cardiac team. At least by the time he was admitted to Downpatrick Hospital, he had learnt to leave the monitors in place! As soon as Uncle Billy regained a sufficient measure of good health, he returned to his home in Belfast, rejoicing, not only in a physically recovered heart but also in a spiritually renewed heart.

Lavinia's diary for May 1983 contained one rather poignant entry, it simply said, *"Lost a baby. Samuel"*.

Just four words that evoke a whole world of pain and tears, the now familiar heartache of shattered dreams, the sorrow felt for a little life cut off before it had even properly begun.

The joy she knew in her two healthy boys did help but it could never begin to compensate for the pain of losing another one. Little Samuel was her third loss, named and remembered, even though the pregnancy lasted for only fourteen weeks.

By July she had only just begun to recover her strength after the miscarriage, when she agreed to take in a baby called Avril, whose mother Rosemary was suffering from post-natal depression. Having a baby in the house was such a joy to Lavinia and her spirits lifted every time she heard little Avril cooing and gurgling. Being able once again to stroke the soft, fragrant skin of a tiny baby really helped to overcome her sadness at losing Samuel. When Rosemary felt a little better, she also came to Ballee for a while and the two women enjoyed many happy hours together, caring for little Avril.

The summer passed in a haze of sunny days spent drinking tea under the shade of one of the trees in the garden; taking time to listen to Rosemary, crying when she cried, laughing when she laughed; watching her boys playing with the many animals that lived at Ballee; immensely happy to be living in the house of her dreams; fulfilled in the work that God had called her to do, the work of ministering to needy people. She was unaware that soon God would begin again to loosen the soil around her roots, unaware that her time at Ballee would soon come to an end.

But the angel who watched as the shadows passed over her life, who stood guard at the edge of their greyness, and the sweet presence of Jesus, Who had walked with her through the shadows, encouraging her heart to sing even in the darkness, would accompany her on whatever path the Lord God might call her to follow.

Chapter 25 ❧

BEHIND THE FENCE

It was five o'clock in the morning. Lavinia dragged herself out of the mists of sleep to hear Robin announce, "I think God is calling me to Sandes."

In later years she laughed at her immediate sleepy reaction, "Do I have to go too?"

They had come into contact with Sandes through Mark and Heather Farmer whom they met in the Downpatrick church. Sandes is a Christian organisation, which serves the Lord in army camps, providing canteen and recreational facilities as a means of outreach. Mark and Heather were the superintendents of the Sandes home at Ballykinler camp, situated near Tyrella Beach in County Down. They lived in the camp, in one of the homes provided by Sandes. Mark had a real gift for enthusing others about the work and often shared his concerns for Sandes with the church missionary committee of which Robin was a member. For some months they had been praying for a new couple to replace workers who were leaving and Robin found himself (as many others have done before him) being called to answer his own prayers! Having wakened at 5a.m. with a strong sense of God's call, he then found it almost impossible to wait to contact Mark, and rose early to find him and share what God was saying.

By now Lavinia was wide awake and quite apprehensive at this turn of events. Although she was totally in sympathy with the work done by Mark and Heather, she wasn't so sure that she wanted to have an active part in it. She was quite happy to support them and pray for the work but to actually live behind the fence was a different matter altogether. She loved Ballee and definitely didn't want to leave it. How could she bear to leave her "castle", her garden?

So, in the early morning, as she usually did when faced with a problem, she reached for her Bible and sent a quick S.O.S. up to Heaven.

"If this is right, You have to tell me and tell me now."

She instinctively turned to the Psalms and sensed God's word for her in Psalm 16.

"Lord You have assigned me my portion and my cup; You have made my lot secure. The boundary lines have fallen for me in pleasant places, surely I have a delightful inheritance."

As she read the words "boundary lines" she could see in her mind's eye the high wire fence which clearly marked the perimeter of Ballykinler Camp and was reassured that whatever her fears about the situation, God had promised that those boundary lines would enclose pleasant places. And so her heart was at peace.

They moved to Ballykilner in October 1985. In the last few days at Ballee, Lavinia experienced a bewildering mixture of emotions - a deep sadness at leaving Ballee but also an increasing excitement at what lay ahead. She walked through the rooms of the old manse, rooms that now held the most precious memories of singing and laughter and tears and her own tears fell as she said goodbye. She moved into the garden to gaze on the trees under whose shade she had rested so many times and grieved that life had to change.

At the same time there was tremendous excitement at the thought of what lay ahead - the opportunity to have a significant input into the lives of young soldiers and the officers who commanded them; the possibility of building relationships with their wives and children; the anticipation of forging a close bond with Mark and Heather.

They had intended to move gradually over a couple of weeks but the first weekend that they brought some of their belongings to Ballykinler, they decided just to stay. It felt good to be there and the "tin hut" (so called because of its corrugated iron walls) to which they were assigned, already felt like home. The boys were thrilled to have other children to play with - Claire and Sarah, Mark and Heather's girls - and soon the four of them were running around outside, happily playing together. After a while, Robin interrupted their adventures and gathered them all into the front room to pray for God's blessing on their new house and new way of life.

Tober the cat settled in very quickly. Over the years at Ballee, all the other animals had died or been given away. Duffy went to live with someone who liked to hunt and it was hoped that he would learn to put his retrieving instincts to good use!

The boys also settled into their new schools and Robin and Lavinia began to learn the different routines of life in an army camp. They soon discovered that much of their service consisted of very practical work. Making and serving food accounted for a large part of the day. Breakfast was served from half past seven in the morning, snacks were taken out in the Sandes van to the soldiers who were on the ranges, lunches and teas had to be prepared, cooked and served. Tables had to be wiped, floors had to be mopped, toilets had to be cleaned, money had to be counted, supplies had to be bought and somewhere in the midst of all this activity, their underlying purpose had to be fulfilled - to bring Jesus to the soldiers.

Lavinia had her own special way of doing this - she poured love into people's lives and took great delight in thinking up little ways to demonstrate that love.

"Can I have some toast, please?" asked one of the young soldiers.

"How do you like your toast?" Lavinia enquired.

The question obviously triggered a wave of homesickness and be began to describe in some detail just exactly how his Mum made his toast. Lavinia's heart went out to him for he seemed to be little more than a child dressed up in camouflage gear.

"Sure son, I'll do my best to make it just like your Mum makes it."

Her warmth and her smile warmed his heart, as did the little chocolate bars that Lavinia used to drop in the letterboxes of the officers' wives. She invited soldiers and officers alike to the "tin hut" for an hour or two of family life, making each one feel appreciated and loved. Some of the young single soldiers almost took up residence with them and ended up calling Lavinia "Mum."

The four of them became involved in all sorts of activities in order to build bridges with the soldiers. Lavinia joined a shooting club, which she thoroughly enjoyed and gave guitar lessons. She often joked that they played everything in G because that was the only key she knew! She and Heather began an aerobics class with the soldiers' wives and worked together in a Saturday club for the children of the camp. Robin introduced a lunch time spot in the Sandes canteen, called the Word at One. In order to create an interest in this, he used to carry a cross into the canteen at one o'clock and then, when he had everyone's attention, he would speak to those who had gathered for lunch. Mark was enthusiastic about all these ideas and used to encourage them by saying, "If God wants you to do it, go for it!"

So Lavinia's days were filled with activity and busyness and if she ever looked back longingly at the relaxed lifestyle of Ballee, it was only very briefly. She knew that she was where God wanted her to be just then and she had a measure of contentment. One thing she did miss more than anything else and that was the warm Christian fellowship she had known with so many people at Ballee. She missed the singsongs and the time spent in long meaningful conversations about the Lord.

Her only compensation was the close relationship she was building with Heather. She had a special bond with Heather from the first day she met her.

July 1983: *"Last Saturday was our women's outing and Heather really ministered to me. I was tired because I'd been caring for Avril and I just needed to relax and Heather just seemed to know. She hugged me, touched my arms so meaningfully, let me rest my head on her knee. Little things like that make all the difference when you're tired."*

Although they had quite different personalities, the two women worked together, the one's strengths complementing the other's weakness. They had much in common - the rigours of life behind the fence, the joys and trials of motherhood, the desire to open their homes to those in need, the highs and lows of being in full-time service for the Lord, the sweetness of fellowship with the group of believers in the little Baptist Church in Downpatrick. They joined other families from the church on caravanning holidays at Cranfield, rejoiced with them at open-air baptismal services on the seashore and sang with gusto at the evening meetings in a nearby hall.

So it was hardly surprising that when Lavinia needed someone to help her with some crafts, it was Heather to whom she turned. The whole idea of selling crafts began for Lavinia when her friend Kate asked if she would be able to sell some satin and lace photograph frames for her in the Centre. They proved to be very popular, so when Kate stopped making them, Lavinia took over and introduced some ideas of her own. One of these involved filling little hats and baskets with pot pourri. Then someone asked if she would put flowers in the containers and so was born the cottage industry that would later become her main means of support - making silk floral arrangements and selling them at parties in people's homes, in much the same way as the Tupperware parties that were so popular at the time.

Heather and Lavinia also saw it as yet another means of evangelism though they did wonder how the army wives would take to their suggestion of a "God spot" at the end of each evening. Much to their surprise, the words of one tough lady summed up the reaction of most of those who were asked,

"I'd be right honoured to have someone talk about God in my place."

It wasn't easy to talk about God in rooms where the air was smoky and raucous laughter, blue jokes and curses preceded the "God spot." In one house, even the animals seemed to be against them, for the parrot swore and dog scratched at the door as they tried to present Jesus to the women who gathered there.

"If God was in this room tonight," Lavinia would often begin and a hush would descend at the very thought of God entering their world.

"Which of these three things do you think He might say to you? 'You'd better shape up,' 'I'm angry at you,' or 'I love you.'"

No one in all the groups she spoke to ever chose the third alternative and it was such a joy for Lavinia to then spend a few moments telling the women just how much God did love them and how He proved that love by dying on the cross. It might have been a simple message but it was enough. The soldiers' wives didn't need to hear deep theology - they simply needed to know that Someone cared for them, that Jesus would accept them just as they were. Those who grasped the amazing reality of God's unconditional, sacrificial love for them found it to be a life-changing experience.

❧

Chapter 26 🐦

PASSING IT ON ...

The young dark-haired boy in the back of the car jumped up and down excitedly when his mother announced with great enthusiasm, "Look boys, we're nearly there!"

He pulled his little brother over to the window for a better view and with eyes that were sparkling, said, "Look Paul, we're nearly there!"

Paul clapped his hands and laughed loudly. An observer could easily have mistaken all this excitement for something else but the destination anticipated with such eagerness was not the start of a family holiday or even a long awaited day out. The car slowed, then turned into the car park of a church.

Lavinia had never lost the excitement of going to church. As she helped the boys out of the car, then walked up the steps, her heart pounded. To her this was as good as it could get.

It never ceased to amaze her how, as she took her place in the pew, it suddenly felt as though God had sat down too, right beside her. It didn't matter whether she was on her own or not, a sense of God's presence flowed over her. The pew became holy ground.

The knowledge of what God had done for her was sometimes overwhelming. The worship tore at her heart and often tears could be seen rolling down her face as she sang words like these,

"Stay, let me weep while you whisper
Love paid the ransom for me."

On other occasions she felt that she would explode with the joy of it all and had difficulty keeping her feet on the ground. There were times when she found it hard to pull herself back to reality after a church service when people spoke to her. The words of a poem by her friend Sylvia Sandys could have been written to describe her feelings.

"Be reasonable
I am no Mary to sit quietly at your feet
And dream.
I am she who runs wild and fleet
Extreme.
I am the Magdalene

How do I love you then, my Lord?
Supreme.
I love you as she herself loved God -
To the extreme.
As the Magdalene."

Robin and Paul soon caught their mother's excitement about going to church and on Sundays they were always as good as gold because the punishment for being naughty was not being allowed to go the evening service and that was worse than being smacked.

Lavinia looked on the years in Ballykinler as years of nurturing her sons and to her the most important part of the nurturing was not feeding them well or dressing them well but passing on to them something of her love for the Lord, her excitement at going to church, her joy in worship, her dependence on God's Word to guide her life, her simple faith that God would guide her and send His angel to protect her.

She was convinced that these two boys would change their world, their generation and felt that it was her responsibility to do what she could to prepare them for their task. Robin's input into the lives of his sons was different but nonetheless important, complementing Lavinia's rather serious efforts. He encouraged them to do all the things that little boys love to do. He introduced them to fishing and often the three of them spent the whole day along the coastline or cycling for miles around the country roads.

When Lavinia spoke in various churches, she would use stories about her children to illustrate what she was saying and often those who listened would say, "You should write a book."

Her reply reflected the seriousness with which she regarded the rearing of her family, "I'm writing two. I've been working at one for seven years and the other one for nine years. My children are the books that I'm writing at the moment."

She wrote a little "book review" in her diary one summer evening soon after they had moved to Ballykinler.

"Paul is seven now, full of joy and playfulness. There is always a gentle love shining from his eyes as he says repeatedly 'I love you, Mummy.' He says he wants to work with animals or in Sandes. He wants to be a helper. I hope he is a great man for God. I think when God gave us Paul, He knew we needed some humour in our lives. Paul is our beautiful, loving clown."

"Robin is nine but looks older. He is serious most of the time but with a soft heart. He's almost the same size as me and has dark hair just like his daddy's and a nature just the same. I can only catch glimpses of myself in this son. He's clever and gets a lot of A grades. He doesn't seem to have to try too hard. He's very musical. It comes easily to him. Any instrument seems to be within his grasp."

"He finds it hard to show his emotions. Sometimes I don't really know what's going on in his mind. I'll have to try harder with this son. Whenever I'm tired and don't feel like making a bigger effort to dig deeper, I need to remind myself that these are very important years in his life. Robin is the son who makes me take a look at myself more often to see if I'm giving him as much as I should."

"So, my sons, God help me to give you both what you need of me to help you to reach your goals in life and never disappoint you as a

mother. I disappoint myself so much that I don't ever want to do that to you. Looking at my sons today, aged seven and nine made me think that someday they'll be men and the work I put into these buildings of clay is a work that will last for eternity."

Having children of her own gave her an increased sense of history. She often thought of her own mother and Granny Johnston and wondered how they had coped with all the mixed emotions of motherhood - the rush of love a mother experiences as her child runs towards her, the stab of fear when they are ill or in danger, the warm glow of pride when they do something clever. She saw Robin so clearly in young Robin and wondered if Lucy had ever seen James in the way she might have held her head or in her smile. She could only remember Uncle Billy as an adult but her grandmother had looked after him as a boy. She recorded her thoughts on these matters one November evening.

"History repeats itself to make me stand silent and think. Tonight before coming to bed, I went in to check the children. There was Robin, black hair visible over the top of his pillow, just a miniature of his daddy, sleeping soundly, not a care in the world. I then went into Paul's room and there he was, curled up, bedclothes almost covering his face completely. I pulled them down and there in the shadows and darkness, I was looking at Uncle Billy. I thought of my grandmother and how she at night, must have looked in on her two boys, Billy and Jackie, and how she must have wondered what their future would bring them. When she died, Uncle Billy took to drink and almost ruined his life for years. He never married. His mother had been the only woman who had loved him."

"Now he has gone and I am standing here looking at my boys just like my grandmother did some eighty years ago."

Uncle Billy's death took place in the "tin hut" at Ballykinler. He hadn't been well yet again and had come down to spend some time with them. It was during this final illness that Lavinia was given a hint of just how much Uncle Billy's attitude towards her had changed. As she helped him to put on a pullover one day, he remarked, "It's a good thing she had you. What would I have done now without you?"

Lavinia felt a lump in her throat as she looked down at the man who had objected so strongly to her birth, who had not wanted her in his home, who at one time, could hardly bear to speak to her, and she thanked God that she had been able to counter his rejection with the love of Jesus.

He passed away one night soon after that conversation, very peacefully, in his sleep. So Uncle Billy too went to be with Jesus, the One whom he had come to know and love.

When the boys were small, they had often listened to Robin and Lavinia singing as part of the Persuaders group and while they were still very young, found that they too had a talent for singing and playing. They formed a family group in 1986, calling themselves Peaceline because both boys had been born near the peace line in Belfast and also because they believed that Jesus was the only One who could truly bring peace. They sang in local churches but the highlight of the little group's singing career was undoubtedly the opportunity to sing in Canada.

The Canadian visit came about as a result of Lavinia's ongoing contact with Isobel, the cousin with whom she had spent much of her childhood. Lucy had kept up the habit of writing to Isobel and Albert and when she died, Lavinia had taken on the task of letter writing. In 1987 Isobel came to Northern Ireland for a month's holiday and stayed with Robin and Lavinia in Ballykinler. The boys enjoyed having another visitor to stay but couldn't understand why she didn't want to share her big bottle of lemonade with them. Lavinia didn't know how to explain to them that the 'lemonade' was really vodka!

As was her custom with all her visitors, Lavinia took Isobel to work with her. Isobel enjoyed helping in the big kitchen of the Sandes canteen and didn't seem to mind sitting in on the housegroup meetings each Tuesday, or joining Lavinia when she took some of the soldiers' wives to various meetings outside the camp. She found herself drawn to this Jesus whose love she saw so forcibly demonstrated to her every day of her visit and by the end of the four weeks, she was determined to become a Christian once she returned to Canada.

Her first letter brought the eagerly awaited news:
"Well I am Christian now ...."
She told her husband about this new relationship she had
begun but Albert was unimpressed by her talk about Jesus and
His love. Isobel found a church to attend but couldn't persuade
Albert to go with her. She continued to pray that Albert would
meet with Jesus and her prayers were answered in a most
unlikely way, in a most unlikely place. Albert visited a
nightclub where he was enjoying himself watching the dancers
when he heard someone speak his name. He turned round to
see who it was but couldn't work out who had spoken to him.
No one was looking at him, no one seemed to be trying to
attract his attention, yet he knew that he had heard his name
being spoken aloud. He had a sudden overwhelming sense that
God was the One who had called his name and he immediately
left the nightclub, hurried home and told the bewildered Isobel
that he had to become a Christian right there and then. So
Isobel's next letter contained the joyful news, *"Albert is Christian
now ...."*
Robin and Lavinia saved hard and the following summer
spent five weeks in Canada with Isobel and Albert. They sang
in Isobel's church and as other churches heard about the family
group from troubled Ireland, they were asked to sing in these
churches too. It was a wonderful holiday - the long flight in the
aeroplane across the Atlantic Ocean, a new country to explore,
new accents to listen to, new food to taste, new friends to make.
Lavinia couldn't help but compare it to her childhood holidays
- day trips to Donaghadee when Davey Williams was in a good
mood - and her heart was full of praise to God that she and
Robin had been able to provide such a wonderful experience for
their two boys.
The letters continued to cross the ocean between Canada
and Northern Ireland and as the years went by she learnt that
Albert was going to Bible College to train for pastoral work.
God gave them a special ministry to people whose lives had
been damaged by alcohol or drug abuse and eventually one of
Isobel's letters contained a special announcement, *"Albert is
going to be a pastor..."*

When Lavinia read those words, she marvelled at the ways of the God she served, a God who took two little girls from the streets of Belfast, little girls who had known the pain of rejection and violence, had drawn them into His family and had blessed each of them with a ministry to damaged lives. And the angel who watched smiled yet again as he read the words over her shoulder.

He often smiled these days as he watched this young mother passing on her own special brand of spirituality to her sons. She knew that she had been successful when she asked Robin why he always carried a little New Testament in his pocket to school. He looked at her as though to say,

"What a stupid question to ask," then gave her an explanation which delighted her heart.

"It's because I know that's where all the answers are. I just take it out and read it when I need to."

The angel had further cause to smile some years later as he watched a young dark-haired young man pull his wife over to the car window as they turned into a church car park, "Look, Emma, we're nearly there."

He beckoned to his wife to watch Lavinia who was clapping her hands and bouncing up and down with child-like excitement.

"See Emma," he said, "Mum still gets excited about going to church!"

Chapter 27 ❧

TOUCHING LIVES

"I was looking for a divine appointment. I was shocked to find my main appointment was with the grill, cooking bacon sandwiches. By the time I was finished I hadn't the energy for anything divine."

For Lavinia the only truly significant part of the work at Sandes was the opportunity it provided to touch the lives of others. She often felt trapped by the daily grind of the work and grasped every chance she could to interact with the people around her. Many of the letters she received from those who passed through the camp at Ballykinler bear testimony to the way she reached out to others.

"Thank you for being my friend when I felt alone ….."

"I am really excited to have met you and feel extremely blessed to know you."

"So thank you, Lavinia, for your words gave me some peace and reminded me from where and only where, that beautiful peace comes …"

"You have a very special gift in making people feel loved and valuable and in getting to the core of the person - it made me want to 'let go' …"

She still remembers with affection the way in which one of the padres who was leaving, introduced her to his successor, "Oh, this is Lavinia. Mark and Heather are the superintendents - Lavinia is Sandes."

She has always considered his rather extravagant words as the biggest compliment she has ever received.

The new padre, Lindsay Murnock, became a close friend. Theirs was a relationship of mutual encouragement. Lavinia encouraged him in his work among the soldiers and Lindsay encouraged her in fulfilling a secret ambition - to study for her GCSE in English. She had regretted leaving school when she did and had always promised herself that someday she would return to her studies. So the year her son Robin sat his GCSEs, Lavinia, encouraged by Lindsay, sat her GCSE in English. She studied through a correspondence course but took her essays to a tutor in the Technical College for marking. Her tutor was shocked to discover that she didn't know what he meant by a verb but was equally delighted to discover that she had a natural flair for writing. She took the course for only four months, sat the examination with the tutor's class and achieved an A grade. Her tutor naturally tried to encourage her to try an A-level but for Lavinia achieving a good grade was enough - she had proved that she could be the best in the class.

The little team who worked in Sandes touched each other's lives at a deep level. They fellowshipped regularly together as a housegroup and once a month spent a half night in prayer. They were sometimes tired and discouraged and on one of these occasions Lavinia was able to pass on to the others a scripture that she felt held some significance for them as co-workers. It spoke of four doorkeepers, an image with which they could easily identify. It was enough to restore their vision and encourage them to press on. They were further encouraged by a dream of Robin's and a conviction held by two of their friends in Community of the King that things were going to change at Ballykinler.

The promised change came with the arrival of a new regiment, the Black Watch. Suddenly it seemed as though they had moved into a period of mini revival in the Camp.

Christians from the regiment came to stand with them in their commitment to share the Gospel and together they saw lives change as people put their trust in Jesus. The enthusiastic Mark became even more enthusiastic!

It was during the latter years at Ballykinler that Lavinia experienced the very special way in which women (or indeed men!) who pray together can touch each other's lives. As there was only a morning service at the Garrison Church, Lavinia and Robin had begun to attend the evening services of Community of the King. She was invited to join some of the ladies who met once a week to worship and share and pray together. Over a period of time, the group learnt to trust each other sufficiently to share honestly and deeply and soon the weekly meeting became a very precious commitment.

Lavinia led the worship each week and was particularly careful to pray over her choice of songs and to approach the worship with sensitivity. On one occasion however, no matter how much she prayed, she couldn't get any inspiration at all for the worship. She felt she hadn't lived closely enough to the Lord to hear His voice. Such was the freedom in the group to be honest, that instead of pretending to have heard from the Lord, she told the group the truth and invited them to join her while she sang songs of repentance and submission and surrender. As a result of Lavinia's honesty, others in the group felt free to be honest too and as they worshipped together, the Lord led them all into repentance. What had seemed at the outset to be an admission of failure was actually used by God to introduce a most significant evening for the whole group.

During another worship time, Lavinia was given a picture which would have far-reaching effects for her. The group had sung a song and then lapsed into a long silence. During the silence, Lavinia saw a picture of two women in a room. One of the women was holding a baby and both of them were gazing at the baby with love. She noticed a boy in the corner. All of a sudden, she sensed that she was the baby and the family gathered round was her Catholic family. She had a feeling that they were preparing in some way for her baptism.

She shared the picture with one of the group, a lady called Kathleen Breen, who took it all very seriously and began to ask Lavinia about her early life. Lavinia told Kathleen her date of birth and Kathleen got in touch with the priest of the chapel nearest to Catherine's Row, the last known address of the Bingham family. She asked him if a baby of that name had been baptised there. The priest was very interested in the story and searched the records for that time but found nothing. He was an old priest who had actually known Granny Bingham and Kathleen relayed what he said back to Lavinia, "If I know anything about Maria Bingham, she would have had the baby baptised herself!"

The picture and the priest's words inspired Lavinia to search once more for her Catholic family. In a way, she felt that God was giving her permission to do so. They hadn't tried to trace her family since Robin had gone to Catherine's Row, in the early years of their marriage, only to find that all the houses had been knocked down for new development. At that time they had looked up old Belfast Street Directories but had found so many Binghams that they didn't know how to even begin their search. So the matter had been shelved for nearly twenty years and although they didn't know it, the search would be put off yet again. God's perfect time had not yet arrived. There were still twists and turns in the road to be negotiated and shadows to be passed through that Lavinia knew nothing about at that time.

One thing she did know - she had a very strong sense that her time in Sandes was over, that she needed to move on to something else. This presented a problem, of course, for Robin was still deeply involved in the work. The restlessness and frustration that resulted made Lavinia's final year in Sandes a rather unhappy one. In the end they decided that one possible solution to the difficult situation would be to invest in a home of their own outside the camp. They bought a little house in Kilkeel and were looking forward to spending some time there. On their very first holiday in the new house however, something happened that would throw all their plans into disarray.

Chapter 28 ❧

HOMESICK FOR HEAVEN

Lavinia woke early on the first morning of her holiday. It was a lovely July morning and she should have been feeling on top of the world. She was on holiday in their new house and she was looking forward to adding the little touches that would turn it into a home.

She had just celebrated her fortieth birthday at the end of June, the two boys were off school for the summer so there were no lunches to make, no uniforms to wash and no homework to supervise, but something wasn't quite right. She had no energy, despite all the rest she had been taking, she felt nauseous and began to think that she had a tummy bug. As the days went by she realized that there was something very familiar about the way she felt and wondered if she might be pregnant. Despite her love for little babies, the thought totally dismayed her. She could think only of the problems - she was forty years old; the boys at fourteen and sixteen, were almost reared; it had been seven years since the previous pregnancy, which had resulted in a miscarriage after a long and difficult labour. She had vowed

at that time that she would never go through it again. She felt
that she didn't have the inner strength to face either a birth or a
death. Her distress was so great that she phoned Heather and
asked her to go down. Heather listened to her, held her and let
her cry.

They decided that the best thing to do would be to phone
Dr Erskine, the consultant at Downpatrick Hospital. He was
most helpful and immediately said, "Come over to my home
today."

Robin and Lavinia made their way to his home where he
chatted to them and suggested doing a scan the next day at the
hospital. The scan confirmed that she was eight weeks
pregnant. His words of congratulations went a long way
towards changing Lavinia's attitude to the pregnancy.

"Just enjoy it," he said and from that moment she resolved
that she would do just that. She had an appointment for a scan
every week with Dr. Erskine, who recorded the scans on video
for her. When she reached eleven weeks, she asked if she could
be taken in to hospital and the doctor agreed to admit her. By
this time her attitude had changed so much that she would have
done anything to keep the baby, but even so, the possibility that
it might die was on her mind and she was conscious of trying to
prepare herself for its death, trying desperately to avoid the
pain of what had hurt before.

Lavinia quite enjoyed the weeks that followed. Since her
livelihood now depended on it, she brought some of her craft
work into hospital with her and entertained the rest of the ladies
in the ward by giving impromptu classes in dried flower
arranging. The women got to know one another well, there was
a lovely atmosphere on the ward, and to Lavinia's delight, they
all settled down on Sunday evenings, to watch Songs of Praise
with her.

In the fourteenth week of her pregnancy, she began to feel
a little unwell and the doctors thought that it might be the result
of her underactive thyroid. She thought no more of it and went
off quite happily for her scan on the Thursday of that week. She
looked over at the screen once again to marvel at their ability to
see the outline of the baby inside the womb. She noticed that

the doctor kept going over and over the same area and glanced at his face in puzzlement. That quick glance at his face was all that was needed - she knew immediately that something was wrong. When she looked back at the screen she realised that there was no heart beat - the white dot was still.

For one agonizing moment she held her breath, then Dr Erskine said, "Sorry, it's gone."

The sister immediately took her hand and said just the right thing,

"Now Mrs Abrol, don't you know that wee soul's with the Lord. What name have you picked?"

But no amount of comforting words could stem the tide of utter despair that swept over her. Far off, in the distance, she could hear a woman howling and howling, then all at once she realised that it was herself. The doctor left just then saying that he would have to do the scan again to confirm it.

The sister brought a phone to her and she managed to get through to Robin in Sandes. It was difficult to get the words out to tell him that the baby had died. Robin assured her that he would come up as soon as he could but he was on duty and couldn't leave work until someone relieved him.

Meanwhile the sister stayed with Lavinia and encouraged her to cry. When Dr Erskine came back into the room he told Lavinia that he would have to put her into labour. She was immediately transported back to the horror of the last miscarriage and fear gripped her.

"Oh no, Doctor, I really had a bad time before. I was in awful pain and no one would give me any pain relief. I couldn't face going through that again."

Dr Erskine was immediately reassuring, "You'll not have a bad time. I'll make sure of that."

He pulled out his prescription pad and wrote up prescriptions that would cover any level of pain. He handed them over to the sister and Lavinia's fear began to recede.

As soon as the doctor left, the sister asked, "Do you want me to tell the women on the ward?"

Lavinia gratefully accepted her offer, so thankful to have such a sensitive nurse looking after her. She seemed to anticipate Lavinia's needs, to know when to speak and when to be quiet, to make appropriate suggestions.

"I'm going to make a pot of tea," were her next words, "You come up when you're ready and we'll all have tea together."

Lavinia walked slowly out of the scan room into the nearest bathroom, her whole body a picture of despondency. She sat in the bathroom in total despair, trying to cry quietly so that others wouldn't overhear. All her dreams had been crushed once again. She had to face yet another loss and it seemed to her, as she sat, overwhelmed by grief, that her whole life had been just full of loss.

She was too preoccupied with her grief to even cry out to God and yet He was there and chose at that moment to reveal Himself to her in a wonderful way. As she opened the bathroom door to walk out, it seemed as though the whole bathroom was bathed in light. She took her hand off the door handle, turned round and sat on the bath. She had a strong sense that God was there, that this could prove to be a special moment. She began to sing a hymn, written by a composer who had known the pain of loss.

"O Love that wilt not let me go,
I rest my weary soul in Thee;
I give Thee back the life I owe,
That in Thine ocean depths its flow
May richer, fuller be.

O Light that followest all my way,
I yield my flickering torch to Thee;
My heart restores its borrowed ray,
That in Thy sunshine's blaze its day
May brighter, fairer be.

O Joy that seekest me through pain
I cannot close my heart to Thee;
I trace the rainbow through the rain
And feel the promise is not vain
That morn shall tearless be.

O Cross that liftest up my head,
I dare not ask to fly from Thee;
I lay in dust life's glory dead
And from the ground there blossoms red
Life that shall endless be."

She sang softly so that others wouldn't hear and think that she had lost her sanity and all the while she sang, God's presence filled the room and the God who had reached out to her in this special way on another occasion when she prayed for her firstborn son, now surrounded her with His felt presence as she grieved for the loss of this son. As she sang those beautiful words of George Matheson's, she began to think, "This isn't what it's about. It's about Heaven. There will be a place where there'll be no more crying."

In a strange way the thought of a tearless morning in the Heaven that always remained close to her heart, comforted Lavinia and the sadness and distress she felt lessened just a little. She often felt homesick for Heaven and at that moment a wave of longing swept over her. She walked out of the bathroom different - still broken and crushed, but different. She sensed that there was a purpose, a significance in this loss and she would hold on tightly to that sense of purpose in the days that lay ahead.

As she walked back into the ward, the other ladies came over one by one to hug her and to offer their sympathy.

"This shouldn't have happened to you," one of them said, for even in the short time they had known her, they had come to love her. They sat together in the ward, drank the tea the sister had provided and cried with Lavinia until it was time for her to be induced.

Realising that she would need a strength beyond her own to endure the next few hours, she phoned Kathleen to ask her prayer group to pray. As three of them were also expecting babies, they found it difficult to decide who should go to stay with her through the labour. In the end they agreed to send Roseanne, even though she was pregnant. It was a good decision for Roseanne had lost a baby the year before and had also had a miscarriage. In many respects, she had earned the right to be there. She knew exactly what Lavinia was going through.

For much of the time they walked up and down the corridor and even in the midst of her pain and distress, Lavinia's sense of humour came to the fore when she realised that Roseanne was busy praying in tongues on one side of her and a Catholic nurse was busy praying to the saints on the other side!

"What about pain relief?" the nurse kept asking, "Do you want me to give you something for the pain?"

"No I'm alright yet," Lavinia would reply, "I want to keep it for when the pain gets really bad."

But God worked a miracle for her and the pain never got bad enough for her to need the prescriptions that had been written up for her. Of all the labours she had been through, it was the easiest and the quickest.

The tears came just as she was about to deliver - a great sorrow came over to her at the thought that it wasn't right for this baby to be born just then. She squeezed the nurse's hand hard, the junior doctor very tenderly wiped away her tears and the baby was delivered.

"Was it a boy or a girl?" she enquired

"A wee boy," came the reply. "You've got visitors outside," the nurse continued, "do you want to see them?"

Lavinia couldn't face seeing anyone just at the moment but it was a comfort to know that Heather and Roseanne were there, thinking of her and praying for her. The nurse took the little body away and Lavinia was prepared for theatre.

By the time she came out of theatre again, Robin had arrived and Dr Erskine spoke to him and reminded him about the video that had been taken of the early scans.

"Now you see that video?" he said. "Put it away in a dusty corner. Some day you might be able to look at it. I'm really sorry about the way it has turned out."

Back on the ward, Lavinia came round to find another of her prayer group friends, Julia, waiting to visit and share her pain. In spite of the fact that it was twelve o'clock at night, the hospital had allowed her to come in. The love of her friends was a great support to Lavinia in her distress.

The nurse on duty that evening, Mary Rice, kept coming in all through the night. She assured Lavinia that she was sitting with the baby, now called Erskine after the doctor who had been so good to her. Mary had placed him in a little box, collected flowers from the various vases on the ward to put all around him, in case Lavinia wanted to go to see him. Lavinia's grief was too raw to face it that night but it meant a lot to her to know that the little body was being treated with such respect. Mary always talked about him by name and that was important too. When she brought Lavinia some literature about the Miscarriage Association, she explained that she had been doing some research for a project on miscarriage and had sent to England for the literature. Although Lavinia thanked her and accepted it, she felt that she would probably never need it. It might however be helpful to some of the girls at the army camp.

Next morning she went to say her goodbye to Erskine. Although Heather and Jeannie were there, visiting her, she decided not to ask them to go with her to the room where the nurse had placed him. It was a lonely time and the tears flowed freely as she bent over the tiny but perfectly formed body of her little son. She counted his fingers and toes and thanked the Lord for him and the weeks she had carried him. When she returned to the ward, Heather and Jeannie wept with her and did their best to comfort her.

When Dr Erskine arrived in the ward the following day for his ward round, he gently reached out to touch her feet as he passed her bed. It was a gesture that said to Lavinia, "I care" a gesture that symbolized for her the excellent care she had received from everyone who looked after her in Downpatrick Hospital. When he told her that she could go home, the thought suddenly hit her very strongly that there was nothing left to keep her there - no need to lie still or to be careful to protect the longed-for baby.

Later that day, in the tin hut at Ballykinler, she took down the family Bible and read the names she had written over the years.

"Lavinia Catreen …
Robin …
Paul …
Baby Abrol …
Samuel …"

She recalled the day she had asked Robin if they could have six children and she thought,

"Well we did have six. Two of them are with us, the other four are in heaven." Then she slowly added the sixth name.

"Erskine George Antony Abrol."

❧

Chapter 29 ❧

THE VALLEY OF THE SHADOW

Lavinia walked the valley of grief for four months. She had never been allowed to grieve for the other babies she had lost, so in a very real sense, she was grieving for all four losses. There was also a sense of finality about this miscarriage that deepened the sadness and removed hope - she was now at an age where child bearing was less and less likely so she couldn't even find comfort in the possibility of another pregnancy.

She couldn't read very much, or write or pray. No longer did the boys come home from school to find their mother singing while she worked in the house, for she had lost her song. When she could read, she concentrated on the psalms because David talked a lot about tears - he was a writer who knew about sorrow and suffering. She felt a great affinity with the children of Israel who hung up their harps on the willow trees because they found it impossible to "sing the Lord's song in a strange land."

Lavinia gave herself four weeks then went back to work in Sandes. She cooked meals, cleaned tables, swept floors, trying to establish the same routine as before but found it all such a struggle. Hard work had helped to pull her out of grief before but this time was different. As each day went by it became harder and harder to do anything. She had no heart in it any more, no enthusiasm, no smile.

Her tightly-held control finally snapped in the most unexpected way. She was serving at the counter when a policeman asked for a cup of tea. His need somehow seemed so trivial compared to hers, something, broke inside and she ran out crying. From that moment on, she moved slowly from grief into depression.

She cried all day, every day. As soon as her feet hit the floor each morning, the crying began. She cried while she peeled potatoes at the sink, wailing in anguish like a Middle Eastern widow. She cried while she did her crafts, taking no joy in the beauty of the arrangements she created. She walked from room to room like a lost soul, searching in vain for something that she would never find. At her lowest point, death became a welcome prospect.

Eventually she went to the doctor who diagnosed postnatal depression and prescribed anti depressants. She took the tablets, asked all her friends to pray for her and waited for God to do a work of grace in her life once more. Although she was empty inside, devoid of any ability to worship or respond to her God, she never lost her faith in His ability to lift her out of the awful pit in which she found herself. She held on to the memories of what He had done for her on former occasions and often recalled the amazing sense of His presence that she had known in that hospital bathroom. She read a verse in Isaiah chapter 5 that just seemed to leap off the page to catch her attention:

"I will give you the treasures of darkness, riches stored in secret places."

"What possible treasure could there be in this darkness?" she wondered to herself. So far there hadn't been too much treasure, just awful pain but she trusted her God and waited for the treasures to be revealed.

Robin and she decided to sell the house in Kilkeel and buy a little bungalow near the army camp in Ballykinler. This meant that Lavinia was able to live outside the camp, as she had longed to do for the previous year and yet Robin was close enough to continue working at Sandes for a few more years.

Settling in to their new home was a form of therapy for Lavinia. She tried to keep busy, redecorating two of the bedrooms and gradually transforming the house, now called 'Robin's Nest' into a warm, welcoming home.

After much heart searching they decided that Lavinia would not go back to work at the camp but would concentrate on building up her own floral designs business once she began to feel better. She did retain an interest in Sandes and was thrilled when some years later her younger son Paul joined the team at Ballykinler, working there until soon after Mark and Heather left to take up a pastorate in England.

"Our Paul followed our footsteps into the work of Sandes. We did not know that Paul would carry on where we left off and do it even better. He relates well to the soldiers. He's their age. He takes them out, brings them here for meals, goes to the bank for them, sits with them in the centre to all hours in the morning as they share their sorrows and joys with him. He is now suffering the pain of a regiment moving on - the loss of dear friends, separated by an ocean. This is the world of Sandes and has always been so. This is the price. To me it was the highest price of being a Sandes worker. Now Paul sets about the task of making new friends, searching out people to whom God leads him, touching lives with his life which carries the living God, being a friend even when others let him down. Although I've been gone from the work for five years now, I feel more involved than ever because of this boy."

It was as she walked this valley of brokenness and despair that God chose to give her a promise which almost seemed an impossibility. The ladies in her prayer group joined the men's group for a meeting and Lavinia went along to it, even though she was in very bad form and didn't enjoy the meeting at all. She felt out of it, as though the others, who were enthusiastically worshipping and praying together, lived on an entirely different planet. Roseanne's husband, Lawrence, was one of the group and afterwards he told Lavinia that God had given him a word to pass on to her.

"Your name is going to be known," he said. "It will be a good name to know and people will use your name all over the land."

Lavinia looked at him in amazement. She thanked him for his encouragement but couldn't see how anything he had said would ever be true of her. Who would want to know the name of a sad, down hearted woman who felt dead inside? Like Mary of old, she kept what had been said in her heart and wondered about it from time to time. Maybe at some time in the future, she would get her song back and have a singing ministry again? She never for a moment imagined that the very area in which she had been so broken, the loss of her babies, was the area that would prove to be the fulfilment of God's word to her through Lawrence. God's grace is such that He often doesn't wait until we are on our feet to get in touch with us but instead reaches out even if we have neither the strength nor inclination to reach out to Him.

She had come across the literature for the Miscarriage Association one day and thought that it might be a good idea to make contact with them to ask for information so that she could help others when she felt better again. She discovered that the work had just begun to develop in Northern Ireland. There had been no such association when she had lost the other babies. The girl in charge explained the way they operated and said that they hoped to appoint a development officer soon who would be in touch with her.

Some time later, just as Lavinia was beginning to move out of the darkness of her depression, the Miscarriage Association contacted her to see if they could pass on her telephone number to a man who was looking for help. She agreed and went along to some of the meetings arranged by the Association. It soon became apparent that miscarriage counselling was work to which Lavinia was especially suited. Those who met her and listened to her speak took note of her compassion and her understanding. It wasn't long before she was asked to act as the secretary for the group and her telephone number was used on the literature for the Northern Ireland helpline.

So began a ministry in which Lavinia is still involved - child bereavement counselling. She operates a 24 hour helpline from her home and the phone rings at all hours of the day and night. Her number is passed on to those who have lost babies by nurses and doctors and to Lavinia it is very significant that often the first words they say are, "Your name was passed on to me by …"

Each time she hears those words from the other end of a telephone line, she thinks back to the days when someone in a prayer group told her, "People will use your name all over the land."

In her work for the Association, she is often invited to address groups of nurses and doctors in hospitals as part of their training in bereavement counselling. She sometimes finds it hard to believe that she really is standing in front of eminent physicians and surgeons, telling her story and advising them about the best way to interact with bereaved couples. What amazing things God can do with a young Shankill Road girl and her simple faith! At gatherings such as these Lavinia usually carries in her pocket the little ten - commandments bracelet that was so precious to her as a young Christian in difficult circumstances. She touches it now and then to remind herself of her humble beginnings and her heart sings out in praise to the God who has walked by her side. She could never have imagined the rich treasure that has been gleaned from the pain of her darkness.

As the months passed, she became increasingly confident that her walk through the valley of this shadow was coming to an end. She could begin to see a little light in the darkness but her song had not yet been restored - there was no singing in the shadow. Because her life had always been so full of song, there was now a very real sense of something being missing. She tried to sing but the joy had gone.

It took a change of church and a renewed acquaintance to bring back the music. Robin and she began attending Ballynahinch Baptist Church soon after she lost the baby. They appreciated the welcome they received and the warm fellowship of the people and joined the church soon afterwards. When she shared with the Pastor, Hadden Wilson, about the miscarriage she had suffered and the depression she was going through, he advised her to get to know some of the women in the church, confident that they would be able to draw along side her and minister to her.

On one of her early visits to the church, she had caught sight of a face from her past, Maisie Adamson, now Maisie Duncan. Maisie had also been on the road in a singing ministry when the Persuaders were just beginning to sing around the Province. The two women hadn't met for over twenty years but as they talked together, Lavinia began to wonder if this was one of the women God intended her to get to know.

She had sensed all those years ago that Maisie had a special relationship with Jesus, noting her impressions of their first meeting in her diary.

"We sang at Enniskillen tonight. It was a Gospel concert. Met a girl called Maisie Adamson. There was something special about her. We talked in the wings before she went on. She said her nerves were wrecked yet when she went on to the stage, her voice betrayed none of what she was feeling. Our group listened as she plucked her guitar and sang, her body swaying to the rhythm. As she sang the words of the song, she forgot the people around and was lost in worship. A hush fell over the place as the story of the cross unfolded. When she came off and we took our place on stage, it felt as though we were standing on holy ground. Maisie was anointed. It was obvious that her relationship with the One she was singing about was special. She knew Him well. I would have loved to have had time to get to know her..."

She looked now at the disabled daughter Maisie was holding on her knee and she knew that here was someone else who had also known sorrow, who might be able to understand her distress.

They agreed to meet for coffee in Maisie's home but the coffee went on into lunch and the lunch went on into afternoon coffee as they talked and shared together. Their sharing was at a deep level and Lavinia could see from Maisie's eyes that she did understand so she was able to experience the wonderful freedom of really unburdening herself. Maisie talked of the pain she had felt when Sarah was born but was also able to encourage Lavinia, by telling her how she had lost her song for a long time but eventually God had brought her to the place where she had learnt that it was possible to sing in life's shadows.

When they finished talking, Maisie suggested, "Why don't we go into the drawing room and sing?"

She had no way of knowing that the very suggestion of singing made Lavinia want to curl up and die so she led the way to the piano, sat down and began to play and sing. Lavinia joined in, a little uncertainly at first but soon her voice was blending with Maisie's, adding harmony to the melody line. God chose to inhabit their praises and soon what had begun as a time of singing became a time of worship. In the silences between the songs, they knew the reality of His presence with them.

"I'd love you to join our worship band in the church," said Maisie quietly.

Lavinia's immediate response was to draw back.

"Oh Maisie, I can't! I'm empty. I've nothing to give."

"Well, pray about it," encouraged Maisie, "I think it's right."

Lavinia left the house that day happier than she had been in months. She was anxious to know the Lord's mind on the matter and spent some time with her well-worn Bible that evening. She could hardly take it in when every scripture she read seemed to have something to do with singing. It wasn't long before she was totally convinced of the Lord's will for her and phoned Maisie that same evening.

"You'll never believe this," she said, "but the answer is 'yes'."

Even with such a clear word from the Lord, it still wasn't easy. The first few times she joined the group she was very conscious that she was singing out of brokenness. Each time before she went out to sing she prayed, "Lord, give me Your peace for my pain and Your joy for my sorrow, for I have nothing."

Little by little, the song came back to her heart and this time she sang a richer, deeper song because of the depth of sorrow she had been through. There was a new joy in her worship that no longer depended on her external circumstances. She had indeed learnt to sing in the shadow and the God of abundance poured out joy in abundance on her head. Not only did she want to sing - she wanted to dance, to give expression to this new-found joy in whatever way she could.

When Maisie was invited to lead worship at Focusfest, a large interdenominational women's conference, she asked Lavinia to be part of her group. It was such a joy to stand on the platform in the Diamond of the New University of Ulster and watch the faces of thousands of women from churches all over Ireland as they were led in worship. For some, it was the first time they had experienced the difference between singing and worshipping and it was a wonderful privilege to see their faces light up as they entered into the reality of true worship, encouraged by Maisie to reflect on the greatness and faithfulness of their God.

And so in the years following her last miscarriage and the great shadow of depression that had resulted, Lavinia began to give back something of what God had given her. Through her work with the Miscarriage Association, she was able to pass on to other damaged lives some of the lessons she had learnt through her difficult experiences. Through her involvement in worship bands, she was able to communicate some of the tremendous joy that can be found in worship.

When the founder and director of Christian Guidelines, Michael Perrott, came to speak in Ballynahinch Baptist Church, she discovered yet another way in which she could give something back as a thank offering for all God had done for her.

Lavinia with the Focusfest Band.

Michael spoke about his work and the great need there was in Northern Ireland for trained Christian counsellors. There was simply not enough people to talk to those who needed help. She sensed God's call in the service and knew that He was asking her to give some of her time to this work. She had felt for some time that counselling was a neglected aspect of the ministry of the Christian Church. In Christian circles the impression was often given that Christians shouldn't have problems and so they felt ashamed to admit that they did have problems. She told Michael after the service that she would be interested in counselling but Robin was ill at that time and it was some years later before she was able to begin her training. She hopes that while she completes her training, her experience as a child-loss bereavement counsellor will be an area of special expertise in which she will be able to serve in Christian Guidelines, helping others as they also walk through the valley of shadows in their own lives. She can, with confidence, reassure them that there is hope even in the most difficult of situations, that when God is allowed to do His work and apply His grace to their circumstances, His light shines in the darkness and His love brings peace to their troubled hearts.

Chapter 30 ❧

WE'VE FOUND THE CHILD

Pat Bingham heard the doorbell ring but let her youngest son, Hugh answer it. She didn't recognize the car outside the gate and wondered what the stranger might want.

"Do the Binghams still live here?" the man asked.

Hugh wasn't sure how to reply - living in Twinbrook had taught him to be wary of strangers so he called to his mother, "There's a man here."

Pat went to the front door where a pleasant but foreign - looking young man was standing, looking a little unsure of himself.

"I'm making a few enquiries," he began. "My wife thinks she might be related to your family. James Bingham is the person I'm trying to find."

"Well now," said Pat, "I'm married to Thomas Bingham. I think you'd better talk to Thomas himself."

She and Hugh chatted for a moment or two and decided that the best thing to do would be to take the stranger over to the golf course where Thomas was playing that evening. The only available transport was Hugh's milk float so the two of them set off for the Old Dunmurry Golf Course. Hugh wasn't sure what to think and even wondered if it was possible that his father might be the stranger's wife's father too!

Thomas, meanwhile, was enjoying his round of golf for it was a fine, though cold March evening. He had just reached the 5th green, which was situated close to the road, near a roundabout when he heard his son calling to him and looked up to see the milk float parked nearby.

"There's a man looking for you," shouted Hugh.

Thomas came over to see who was looking for him but didn't recognise the stranger with Hugh and wondered what was going on.

When the stranger asked for James Bingham, Thomas became rather confused. He immediately thought of his nephew, James, Brigid's eldest son. Her maiden name of course had been Bingham but because she had married a Bingham, her children were Binghams too. Thomas couldn't think of any other James Bingham and couldn't understand how his nephew could possibly be this man's wife's father. Suddenly it dawned on him that his brother Seamus would have been known as James in Protestant circles and everything began to fall into place.

"Now I know what you are talking about," he said. The round of golf was forgotten as he threw his clubs into the back of the milk float and hurried home to find out more from the stranger, who was, of course, Lavinia's husband, Robin.

As they rode home together, he became more and more sure that Robin was talking about his brother Seamus, despite the fact that Robin called his wife Lavinia and Thomas remembered the little baby as Mary Kathleen. It was soon all straightened out as they sat together in Thomas and Pat's comfortable front room and talked long into the night.

Robin told them the story of the search for Lavinia's father and how they had tried various avenues but had been disappointed. They had then decided, just recently, that it might be helpful to know when her grandmother had died, so Lavinia had spent a day in the offices of the Belfast Telegraph, going through hundreds of death notices, looking for her grandmother's name. The notices had given her the date of the death, so, armed with this information, she had gone to the Public Records Office to obtain a copy of the death certificate. She had been thwarted once again because the whole system had been computerised and she hadn't known how to retrieve the information she needed. Eventually she had phoned the office and had been advised to send in the information she had and a cheque for the certificate, which had then been posted out to her. From that certificate they had found Thomas' address and they had wondered whether or not they should try to make contact. When Robin asked where Seamus was now and how they could get in touch, there was a little silence and Thomas looked at Pat before he replied, "I'm afraid Seamus died some years ago."

Robin's heart sank. He knew Lavinia would be so disappointed. It was a possibility that had not crossed their minds. Lavinia had been concerned that her father might not want her and had never thought that he might be dead.

"Oh I'm really sorry," he said slowly.

"He died nearly ten years ago in Leeds," Thomas explained, "he developed cancer and died in St. James' hospital."

Bit by bit, the story of Seamus and Lavinia was pieced together. Robin explained how Mary Kathleen had become Lavinia and Thomas tried to remember all he could about the early days of Lavinia's life.

"I was just a boy of sixteen," he recalled, "so I wasn't told very much. I was aware Seamus had done something to bring shame on the family but I wasn't too sure just what. I remember the day Eileen baptised her but in those days you didn't ask too many questions. Margaret-Mary or Eileen would be able to tell you more."

By the time Robin left that night, they had agreed that Thomas would tell the others in his family, that Robin would assure Lavinia of a welcome to the Bingham household and that they would make an arrangement soon to get together. Robin's car had hardly pulled away from the gate before Thomas was on the phone to his brother Oliver and his sisters Margaret-Mary and Eileen.

"We've found the child!" he said to each one in turn.

Margaret-Mary didn't have to ask what child he was talking about. Her thoughts instantly went back to a little girl who had once lived in her home, whose name she would never forget because she had been praying every day for Mary Kathleen, a little girl who was still part of the Bingham family even though they had not seen her for forty years.

Robin, meanwhile, went back to Lavinia with a heavy heart. She had spent the evening feeling sick with a mixture of apprehension and excitement and her heart started pounding when she heard him open the door.

"Well did you see anyone?" she enquired anxiously.

Robin tried to soften the blow but there wasn't any easy way to break the news about her father.

"You have a lovely family. They're dying to meet you. You're gonna love them - but I'm afraid your father's dead."

Lavinia's face crumbled and grief hit her like a flood.

"Ah, he can't be dead!" she cried.

She had prepared her heart for rejection, had prayed for peace to accept whatever reception she might get from her father but she had made no preparation for the news of his death. It was as though he had just died that day and so Lavinia began a period of mourning for a father she had never known and would never now have a chance to meet. All the dreams she had held on to of building a relationship with her father were shattered in an instant and she spent the week that followed grieving for what she had lost. It was a strange grief because she couldn't go to her friends and say, "My father has just died," though that was exactly how she felt and she could have done with being able to lean on the support and sympathy of others. So she brought her sadness to the One who had always understood and poured out her heart to the One who loved her above all others.

It was only when the worst of the pain had begun to subside that she could begin to appreciate the fact that while she may not have found her father, she had found her family.

Realization began to dawn that she had uncles and aunts and cousins and that they wanted to meet her and gradually the joy built up in her heart.

A great family get together was arranged for 2nd April at Thomas and Pat's house. When Lavinia and Robin walked through the door, they were met by a sea of smiling faces. It seemed that everyone who belonged to the Bingham family, except Aunt Eileen, who was ill, had gathered for the celebration, all so excited to meet this new niece and cousin. Lavinia's heart was full as she sat in the middle of her new family - her Uncle Thomas, Aunt Margaret-Mary, Uncle Oliver, who had travelled all the way from Dublin to meet her. One cousin after another came to greet her, "I'm Christine _____, I'm Hugh_____, I'm Gerard _____."

There were smiles and hugs, tears and laughter. When Lucy had died Lavinia had thought herself all alone in the world and she could hardly believe her eyes as she looked around the crowded room - such a large happy family, so many people to get to know. There were so many questions she wanted to ask, so much she wanted to learn but she knew she had to be patient - she had the rest of her life to build relationships with these folks who could fill in the missing gaps in her own life. One thing, though, she couldn't wait to find out.

"Tell me," she begged, "about my baptism. Robin told me you had baptised me as a baby when I was with you."

The picture of her baptism had been the reason why she had renewed her efforts to find her father and so she listened carefully while Margaret-Mary told her about the little group who had gathered round Eileen in the kitchen. As the scene was described to her, Lavinia wasn't really surprised to hear that it had happened just as she had seen it in her picture. God had used it to give her a family and to give her the opportunity to find out about her father.

Seamus had stayed in the Airforce for twenty-two years. He used to return home for funerals and other family occasions. He was a private person who didn't tell his family much about his thoughts or feelings but Thomas suspected that on those early visits home, he had gone looking for Lucy and her little daughter.

"When the troubles were at their height," Thomas told Lavinia, "he'd spend almost a whole day away. When we asked him where he had been he told us he had gone up and down the Shankill Road. It wasn't the safest place for a Catholic to be at that time and we can only think that he was concerned about Lucy and was looking for her and the baby."

Lavinia understood at once why he had never found them for her name had been changed and Lucy's surname had been changed when she married Davey Williams. It brought a measure of comfort to her heart to know that her father had been prepared to risk his life out of concern for Lucy and his child.

She learnt that she had been in effect his only child, for Seamus and Mary had no children of their own, but had adopted two boys. They had lived in army camps for most of their married life but after their final posting in Ballykelly, Seamus bought a van and began a mobile fruit and vegetable round in Belfast. Despite his years of service with the British forces, his two boys were intimidated during the troubles and Seamus and Mary decided to move back to England. He drove a taxi in Leeds until the illness that resulted in his death in 1983.

"Do you have a picture of him?" asked Lavinia.

Thomas and Pat hunted through their family photographs until they found some pictures of Seamus and for the first time in her life Lavinia looked at her father's face. It was a significant moment for Lavinia and she was suddenly filled with a deep desire to know all that she could of this man who had fathered her. The photograph was black and white of course so she began asking about the colour of his eyes and hair. She wanted to know how tall he was and what sort of person he had been and those who sat around her answered her eager questions as best they could.

In the weeks and months that followed Lavinia met up with various members of her new family. She met Aunt Eileen and spent some time with Margaret-Mary. She learnt that her grandmother and aunts had kept in touch with her until she was two years old. She heard for the first time about the presents they had brought to her and their deep sadness when the contact with her had to be broken.

"You know, I think I saw you again," said Margaret-Mary. "I passed Lucy one day in the street and she had a little girl with her. I thought it was probably you but I didn't like to stop her to find out because she might not have wanted to talk to me."

Lavinia discovered that she had inherited some of her traits from the Bingham side of the family. They loved music, many of them played instruments, they had a great sense of family and weren't embarrassed to show affection in hugs and kisses, they cried easily and passed round boxes of tissues at emotional moments. She found out that Margaret-Mary was also very good with her hands and made the same sort of dried floral arrangements as Lavinia.

She learnt too that many of them were deeply devout. Margaret-Mary had spent some time in a convent and still devoted much of her time to personal prayer as well as belonging to a prayer group. Thomas had spent three years in a monastery and looked back on that time as a time when his relationship with God had been deepened by time spent in prayer, meditation and reflection. After he left the monastery and married Pat, he still maintained the disciplines of prayer and meditation and in more recent years had become involved with some spiritual groups.

He had a simple faith in God and had been in situations when he had proved God's faithfulness to him.

"He doesn't let you down," he said in one of his chats with Lavinia and he and Pat proceeded to tell her a story that could have come straight out of her own past.

"When we were first married, we had very little money. We found ourselves one Christmas with no money at all - no money for a Christmas dinner, no money to buy the children presents. The children hung their stockings up but we knew we had nothing to put in them. Then just when we needed it, our parents brought us food, one brother brought presents for the children and other brothers gave us money. No, God doesn't let us down."

And somewhere close by the angel who watched, smiled with delight as he looked at these two people from opposite sides of the divide in Northern Ireland, who in normal circumstances would not have had the opportunity to even talk to one another. A young woman who had grown up on the Shankill Road, who had narrowly escaped being blown up by a bomb planted by Catholics, sitting earnestly discussing God's faithfulness with a man from Twinbrook whose brother had been forced to leave his home as a result of intimidation by Protestants. Reconciliation always delights the heart of God.

Chapter 31 ❧

FULL CIRCLE

The finding of Lavinia's Catholic family was like the completion of a circle in her life and the same year in which she had such joy in finding them, she made another discovery that would eventually lead to another full circle, although it would take her along a much less pleasant road.

It was through Lavinia's work with the Miscarriage Association that she found out about the stillborn plot in the City Cemetery. It was a large plot that had been used for years by the hospitals in which to bury stillborn babies whose parents didn't make the funeral arrangements themselves. Learning about the plot brought back all the bitter-sweet memories of Catreen, her firstborn child. She went once more to the drawer where she kept Catreen's shawl and sat holding it for a little while.

"I wonder what happened to Catreen?" she pondered.

Robin and she had been too young and too sad all those years ago to even ask what arrangements would be made and had assumed that the body would be incinerated. For that reason they had never tried to find a grave.

The next time she had to contact the man in charge of the City Cemetery, she enquired if any record was kept of the babies buried in the stillborn plot.

"Oh yes, Missus, we have records that go back many years," he replied.

"Would you be able to check the records for a name for me?" Lavinia asked.

"That would be no problem at all," she was assured. "What was the name and could you tell me the year and the date?"

"Catreen Lavinia Abrol" Lavinia said, and her heart began to beat faster as she went on to give him the details he needed.

"Just hold on now for a minute. I'll go and check for you."

He came back with the news that, yes, there had been a baby called Catreen Abrol buried in the plot on that date. Lavinia thanked him and put down the phone in a state of shock. Somehow she hadn't expected to be told right there and then and as the full realisation of it all broke upon her, she began to feel as though Catreen's death was taking place all over again. Her daughter had been buried there for over twenty years and no one had known.

The evening she told Robin and they made arrangements to go and visit the grave. They called first of all at the office and the man who was there brought the map of the plot with him and led them through the cemetery to a large area at the far end, an area that was beautifully kept and planted with rows of tall trees. He used the map to guide him to the exact spot where little Catreen was buried. Robin and the man talked together but Lavinia couldn't talk. She so desperately wanted to cry but felt that she just couldn't in front of this man who was a stranger and who wouldn't understand why she was crying over something that had happened so long ago. Then the man turned to Lavinia and told her a little detail, which brought a measure of comfort to her heart.

"You know Missus," he said, "we try our best to keep this plot looking well - the grass is cut regularly all through the summer but if you come up in May and June this grave won't be cut. We're not allowed to cut it because a rare orchid blooms there each year and the conservationists have said that it must not be touched while it is flowering."

The caretaker thought that he was merely passing on an interesting piece of information to this couple who had just found their baby's grave but to Lavinia the words were like a message from a gracious God. In the past twenty two years there had been no one to lay flowers on Catreen's little grave but God had ordained that a very special flower would bloom there each year. It was as though God was whispering to her heart,

"Don't feel guilty about this - I took care of it. I have made this a very special place."

She left the graveside, content that she had at last seen Catreen's grave but surprised by the depth of sadness she felt. She went back again some time later, this time bringing a bunch of love-in-a-mist to tie to the nearby tree. She wondered if the grief would lessen each time she visited but found that it remained just as strong. There was something unfinished about the situation and she couldn't work out what it was.

Two years later Lavinia invited her Pastor, Hadden Wilson, to accompany her to a talk she was giving as the representative of the Miscarriage Association. He listened with a keen interest to her story and on the way home asked her, "Did you tell us everything today?"

Although she had not yet told anyone about finding Catreen's grave and her subsequent visits to it, she now found herself telling him about this most recent painful development. As they talked together, Hadden offered to arrange a private service of remembrance at Catreen's grave. Perhaps it would be a helpful thing to say goodbye properly.

"I'll think about it," she promised, "but I'm not sure if I could bear it."

So scared was she of opening herself again to the pain of Catreen's death, that it was six weeks before she was able to tell Hadden that she would like the service to go ahead. The night before the agreed date was difficult. She felt apprehensive - what if it was all too much and she couldn't cope with the emotion it would inevitably bring?

The winter sun was shining over the cemetery when they arrived the following day, bathing the grass and rows of trees in the stillborn plot in light. It all looked very beautiful, even on this cold January afternoon.

Lavinia and Robin were accompanied by Hadden and Heather, Lavinia's close friend. They stood at Catreen's graveside and Hadden conducted a simple service of remembrance. He read Psalm 139 and mentioned Catreen by name. Then he read a poem written by Paul to commemorate the sister he had never met, "To the One I didn't know."

The one I didn't know
I see her shining face beautiful
A little one so small and never got a chance
But, a chance for what?
A chance for the world to try to corrupt
A godly child
A child of God
A child with God now.
A child I will see when I am reunited with my God
My God, our God
When I go there I will see her
Embrace her and say,
You're the one I didn't know.

Suddenly Lavinia felt arise within her an emotion that she could only describe as joy. She asked, "Pastor, can we sing?"

It seemed appropriate to Lavinia that singing should be included - she and Robin were singers and this was something they could give to the daughter they had never known. They had had no opportunity to give her gifts on her eighteenth birthday but they could give her a song. So while a caretaker leaned on his spade nearby and shook his head in amazement at the strange ways of some people, the four of them joined hands and sang "Ascribe greatness to our God the Rock." Lavinia knew in her heart that she could sing with absolute sincerity, "His work is perfect and all His ways are just."

There had been moments in her life when she could have flung accusations of "unfair, unjust" at the throne of Heaven but Lavinia had never felt resentful or bitter, for the good times with God had far outweighed the trials she had experienced along the road. His work was perfect and her heart rejoiced that she could entrust her life to a God whose plan for her was just.

She left the graveside that day, not sad and confused as she had on other visits but with a sense of completion - it was all finally over. That was where it had started and that was where it ended.

As they sat together later on in a coffee shop in Hillsborough, she realised how appropriate it was to finish the afternoon around a table - equivalent to a meal after a funeral service. She looked across at Heather and thanked God for a friend who cared so deeply for her and who was prepared to share her sorrows as well as her joys. Then she glanced at Hadden and thought how privileged she was to have a Pastor who was sensitive and thoughtful, who had a deep desire to hear God's voice, a man who wasn't afraid of unusual challenges and who rose to them so magnificently.

She still goes back to the stillborn plot, still brings a bunch of love-in-a-mist to tie on the tree but she no longer walks away from the graveside feeling sad. She has come full circle and the sense of completion and closure that she felt on the day of the service still remains.

In her counselling and public speaking, she often encourages women not to run away from their fears but to confront them. Lavinia has proved that, while it may be a painful path to take, in the end it is often the only way in which real healing can take place.

Lavinia has walked in the shadow many times in her life but even in the most difficult situations, has never lost her simple, unquestioning faith in the One who loved her and died for her. She has learnt how to sing in those shadows, though sometimes the only song in her heart was in a minor key born out of pain. She has also learnt to use her shadows, recognizing that often they are the places where God reveals His love and His grace in fullest measure, where He makes His children most aware of the sweet fragrance of His presence. It is always a great joy to Lavinia to pass on to others what she has learnt from living in the shadow, sharing the precious treasure gleaned from the darkness, the "riches stored in secret places."

Chapter 32 ❧

GLIMPSES OF HOPE

The telephone rang in the small hours of the morning and Lavinia stumbled sleepily to the kitchen to answer it.

"851596" she murmured.

The tearful voice on the other end of the line immediately began apologising, "I'm so sorry to ring you in the middle of the night but I had to talk to someone. Your name was passed on to me by the midwife in the hospital. I had to wait until my husband went to sleep. He doesn't understand why I'm so upset. Is it alright to talk to you?"

Lavinia broke in on the rush of words, "Of course it's alright. That's what I'm here for. Now take your time and we'll chat together for a little while. What's your name?"

And the angel watched as Lavinia listened to the story of a distressed woman in another part of Northern Ireland, pouring out all the sorrow and bitterness she felt at the loss of her baby. An hour later Lavinia crept back to a cold bed to try and snatch a few hours or sleep before dawn.

❧

Lavinia climbed the flights of stairs up to the door of the Christian Guidelines Offices. She pressed the buzzer and as she waited to be let in, prayed to the God whose ear was always open to her cry.

"Lord, you'll have to help me now. You know I'm nervous. I need Your wisdom and insight."

She had come to the office to take part in a co-counselling situation with Michael, as part of her counselling training. Her nervousness vanished as she was introduced to the one who had come for help. She could see the pain in her eyes and Lavinia's deep-rooted desire to help the damaged overcame the feelings of apprehension. Both Michael and the counselee sensed the warmth of her heart and her compassion. Her voice was gentle and her eyes were kind as she offered words of comfort and hope.

Helen had been referred to Lavinia by Cruse, to whom she had gone for help when she could no longer work because she was feeling so depressed. When the counsellors at Cruse realized that she needed help in the area of child loss, they suggested that she should go instead to Lavinia. It often takes a long time for grief to be worked through, so for the following year, she visited Lavinia every third Thursday. She had suffered her first stillbirth eleven years previously but as a result of a set of extremely difficult family circumstances, had not had time to grieve properly. Her situation remained difficult and so the opportunity to grieve never came, not even when she lost three other babies in the years that followed.

At first when she came to Lavinia, she was afraid of the pain, afraid when Lavinia gently encouraged her to look back and remember.

"Your losses are like ghosts from the past," Lavinia tried to explain. "They seem to be very frightening but you will find if you take them out and look at them, they will no longer hold any fear for you."

So, little by little, the two women sifted through the pain, often passing each other the box of tissues that always sat on Lavinia's coffee table. Gradually Lavinia noticed that Helen was more relaxed in the sessions and she even heard her laugh now and again. Hope was being reborn for the first time in eleven years.

During their final sessions, Helen told Lavinia that she realized that she would soon have to go back to work. By that stage the two women had forged a friendship and both were sad that the sessions together would end. They have kept in touch with each other since then, meeting now and again for coffee. Lavinia often felt that she received more from Helen that she had been able to give, yet Helen felt that the opposite was true. On one occasion when they met for coffee she told Lavinia, "I don't think I would have got through that last year without you. I could recommend anyone to come to you."

Hope had been restored in Helen's life.

∾

The telephone rang again in the middle of the night.

"Oh my baby's dead, my baby's dead."

That was all the broken hearted woman could say at first.

"Was it your first baby?" Lavinia gently enquired.

"No, I have thirteen other children and no one understands why I'm so upset. They all ask me why I'm crying when I have thirteen others. But it was my baby and now it's dead."

The tears flowed again and for a long time that night, Lavinia listened to her pouring out her grief and distress. Lavinia encouraged her to talk about the death of this special baby, her fourteenth and a little seed of hope was sown, hope that in time the pain would grow less, hope that comfort would be found.

∾

Lavinia had been amazed one evening to receive a phone call from Sister Concilia who was in charge of a bereavement support group in St. Peter's Chapel on the Falls Road in Belfast, asking her to speak to the group on child loss. There was a certain irony in the thought of someone from the Shankill Road, who was now a member of a Baptist church, being invited to speak at a meeting in a parochial house at St. Peters.

Nell was one of the lay people who were being trained to help the bereaved of the parish and she listened to Lavinia's story. She too had known suffering, having lost not only babies but also a seventeen year old son. After the talk, she went over to Lavinia, put her arms around her and the two women cried together. Lavinia will never forget the sensation of feeling Nell's tears and her own trickling together down her neck. Neither will she forget what Nell said to her,

"Lavinia wherever you go, tell them that we all cry the same tears. Tell them the grief feels the same."

Each time that story is told, a spark of hope is lit, hope that one day there will be an end to the tears and brokenness caused by the years of conflict in our troubled land.

Lavinia walked into the lecture hall in the Ulster Hospital. She had been invited to take part in a Bereavement Study Day. As she made her way towards the front, one of the other speakers, a psychologist, came over to speak to her.

"Oh Lavinia," she began, "I have heard your name over and over again. I've been longing to meet you."

Lavinia was struck once again by the reference to her name. God's promise to her was still being fulfilled. She took her seat beside her Pastor, who had accompanied her and began to look at the programme. Her heart sank as she read the names of those who were to take part - a psychologist, a G.P., a minister, a paediatric facilitator for bereavement, all with letters after their names, and Lavinia Abrol, just plain Lavinia Abrol.

The chairman came to speak to her, trying to gain some information for his introduction.

"Have you written any books, Mrs Abrol? Do you have any degrees in counselling?"

Lavinia laughed, "I have no qualifications at all, apart from being the woman who knows what it's like to get the bad news."

Lavinia and Hadden listened with interest to the addresses of the other speakers, as did the rest of the four hundred people who had gathered for the study day - doctors, nurses, hospital chaplains, ministers and priests. Then it was her turn. She prayed quietly as she left her seat.

"Lord help me to share enough to help them grasp the feeling, so that they will learn what they need to learn but not so much that I will be damaged by it."

This is her prayer each time she shares her story, for the retelling of the tale is like picking the tops of the scars that have been left there by the pain. It still hurts to remember but God has been faithful and she has never felt damaged by sharing her story, a fact that she acknowledges each time on the journey home, by singing "Great is Thy Faithfulness".

Confident now that God would help her, she walked to the front and began to speak.

"The rain to the wind said,
You push and I'll pelt
They so smote the garden bed
That the flowers actually knelt
And lay lodged though not dead."

"I know how the flowers felt," she continued. "That's my only qualification for being here today."

As she spoke these words, a hush fell over the room. She told her story and those in the audience were glad that the curtains had not been pushed back after the slides, for the tears flowed down many faces. For three quarters of an hour she spoke and the only sound from the audience was a ripple of laughter now and again when her lively sense of humour came to the fore. She was the only speaker that day who made the audience laugh, the only one who had earned the right to do so. She finished with these words, "It only takes a moment to feel cared for, for the rest of your life. That's the moment you remember, that's what you will talk about - the nurse who was kind, the doctor who touched your hand."

In the silence that followed her talk, she slipped her hand in her pocket to touch her ten commandments bracelet and breathed a prayer of thanks to the God of miracles who once again had enabled her to tell her story without breaking down.

Afterwards the Doctor who had introduced her told her, "Your talk should have come with a public health warning!"

Yet another doctor told her that since he had heard her speak on a previous occasion, he had changed his whole attitude to patients who had suffered child loss.

And so on that study day was born the potential for countless moments of hope in hospital wards all over Northern Ireland, moments when a doctor or nurse or minister would reach out with compassion and understanding to those who have been bereaved.

The angel watched as the three women sat together round the log fire. Friday night had been a special night for some years now, the night when they met as a prayer triplet. A strong bond of friendship had been forged during the hours spent chatting over a cuppa, sharing joys and sorrows, worshipping together and interceding for others.

Lavinia finished telling her two friends about the busy day it had been, full to the brim with miscarriage calls and craft work. "But you know girls," she said and her eyes sparkled as she spoke, "there's nothing I would rather do. I just feel that this is why I was placed on the earth. It's great to know that you're where God wants you to be."

"We should thank God for that," said one of her friends, "I think it's time we started to pray. Lavinia have you a word for us?"

Lavinia began to leaf through her Bible.

"This is one of my favourite verses," she said, as she found the book of Isaiah. "Just listen to this. 'They who wait on the Lord shall renew their strength, they shall mount up on wings like eagles,' Isn't that great? It comes too at the end of the praise song we sing in church - you know the one - The Power of Your Love."

Very quietly, she and her two prayer partners began to sing the words of the chorus,

"Hold me close, let Your love surround me
Bring me near, draw me to Your side,
And as I wait, I'll rise up like an eagle,
And I will soar with You - Your spirit leads me on
In the Power of Your Love."

"That's my hope for the future, girls," she added. "I just long to soar, to get up there above the shadows and be able to see my problems and difficulties from God's perspective. I want you to pray that into my life."

And perhaps the angel who watched, nodded in approval as three heads bowed in worship to the King of Kings, praying that each of them would learn how to soar with God, to move on in their Christian experience to greater intimacy with the God of Heaven. And that same God of Heaven, who takes such delight in His children, chose to draw near to them by His Spirit and in the silence as they worshipped they caught a glimpse, not this time of hope, but of glory.

Part Two ⁓

STILL SINGING
The following chapters have been written by Lavinia.

ACKNOWLEDGMENTS ～

A special thanks to....

Robin my husband....... for his computer skills. Thank you for walking this journey with me for 42 years.

Kerry Julie and Pat...... who typed the manuscript. I appreciate you so much.

Gillian........ who encouraged me to have the book printed again. Your timing was perfect.

Gloria,..... my "amazing editor" who knew where to put all these things ".,-:;!'?(-)" Thank you for your excellent skills as an editor, for giving me so much of your time and walking each page with me. Thank you too for your Godly wisdom and for being my friend.

Gwen....... my minder. Thank you for looking after me on all the journeys that we have taken together. Travelling with you is always fun.

Maisie Hill.....my dear friend. Thank you for displaying Christ so well. My life has been enriched so much because of our friendship.

Robin Jnr, and Paul.....Thank you for letting me share your stories and some of the things that God showed me because of you. You are amazing men.

The Staff at Ambassador for your help and encouragement.

Chapter 33 ❧

ROBIN'S DREAM

One of the greatest joys of my life was mothering my sons. I have snap shots in my mind taken at various stages of their lives. I remember those times very well because each time my mind captured a scene I wanted time to stand still. We all know that it doesn't happen. Little boys grow up and become men, but the snapshots remain within us for the rest of our lives. People often ask, "What are the boys doing now?"

The next few chapters are their stories. When they were young I called them the two books that I was writing. Now they are writing their own stories, they are capturing their own snapshots.

Robin, or wee Robin as he was called to distinguish between him and his Dad, had the call of God on his life before he was born. The sense and touch of God on myself, the day I prayed Hannah's prayer in the church, was such that I was sure he would go into Christian work. A gifted son musically and academically, we watched in amazement as he lifted instruments and played them without any tuition. At 6 years old he was playing violin and piano very well. He just knew how to do it. We just looked on as he would play tunes perfectly on any piano that he found. We did not own one at the time. Soon the house started to fill with instruments to encourage his gift. Easy going is a good description of Robin, never one to make a great fuss or worry too much about anything, but capable of doing many things very well.

When he was in his teens there was a missionary coming to our church to speak. Robin said that he wasn't going. It was unusual for Robin to miss church so I said,

"Why are you not going son?"

"If I don't go, there's no chance of God calling me to be a missionary," he replied.

I smiled. Robin was on the run. I knew he had no chance. He loved God, the church youth fellowship and his Christian friends but Robin had a dream. He was going to be a pilot. It was all that captured his mind and from the age of 11, he had been writing to airline companies about qualifications and training. He had his first lesson when he was twelve. He worked in the nearby fields around us picking potatoes to earn money for flying lessons. His room was like the flight deck of an aeroplane, with posters everywhere.

Then something happened to steal his dream. When he was 17 and studying for his A levels, he had a sight test which showed he had a condition called Non Binocular Vision. He could not see in 3D. He would never be a commercial pilot. I was more upset than he was as we walked out of the optician's. This easy going fellow turned to me and said,

"It's alright. God will heal me or He will have something else for me to do."

Not long after that he was reading a Christian magazine and he saw an advertisement for Mattersey Hall Bible College. Robin knew he had to apply. At first they said there were no vacancies, then someone decided not to go and he got that place. I smiled....... he was now running in the right direction.

At Bible college, Robin met a beautiful girl called Emma. Blond haired, blue eyed with dimples when she smiled, Robin was attracted to her from the start. Robin said that although he

Robin and Emma at Bible College.

was not looking for a relationship being with Emma made him feel alive. I asked Emma to share something about their meeting and how she had felt. She too had gone to College not looking for a relationship because she had watched other couples go through trauma and she did not want to be hurt. She wanted to wait for God's perfect partner. This is what Emma wrote........

"I had heard first hand stories of how Godly women had brought petitions to Father, asking Him for men of a certain character, qualities and attributes. I concluded that I would do the same and refrain from further relationships until I knew Father had provided the person I would spend the rest of my life with. When I made that decision many offers came my way but I chose not to get involved in a serious relationship. It was time for me to attend Bible College. I had surrendered all to Father, in order to follow His plan and purpose for my life and was focused on learning about God's Word. I was content with a "be it unto me" attitude regarding life, ready to handle whatever God's will might be, with grace. I thought I would leave College and help the poor in a third world country, but God had other plans."

"I remember feeling apprehensive the first evening at Bible College meeting a crowd of new people and pondering the new schedule of my life. As all the new students gathered to play ice-breaking games one person in particular caught my attention. My instant observation was how unusually calm and laid back this person was in a new environment. We would go out in groups for long walks and somehow this laid back person and I would always end up together. After many long walks and talks and laughter, this laid back person confessed his feelings towards me. I took a planned trip to Scotland to visit a friend which gave me time to think and pray about the situation. As I gazed at my list of characteristics and attributes I had petitioned to Father so many months earlier, I realized the laid back person fitted all the criteria. God confirmed this to me over the next two weeks through the same scripture in three different locations. I knew God was speaking a direct message to me and if I was not careful, I could let my fears of being hurt make me miss what was God's plan for me. The laid back person was Robin - God's good plan for my life."

"Robin had informed me casually that we would live in Canada one day as it had made such an impression on him as a little boy. I assured him that I would never move to such a place, Lord willing. Robin knew Father would change my heart if it was His plan. Father did."

Two years into Bible College they married. After graduation Robin took a Post Graduate Certificate in Education at St Martin's Lancaster. His first teaching job was in Kent. His next one was in Longridge, close to Lancaster. Our first grandchild, Torben, came along shortly after that.

Robin had always been interested in leading church worship and a part-time worship director's job came up at St Thomas's Lancaster. Robin got the job in this wonderful vibrant Anglican Church and blossomed under the leadership of Peter Guinness, the Vicar. He also worked in supply teaching.

Our second grandchild was born, Katriona, called after our still-born daughter Catreen. I shall always remember the day Robin phoned and said, "Mum, we've had a baby girl. 8lb 7ozs. She has a head full of dark hair, so special, and reminds me of how my sister must have looked when she was born. Would you mind if we called her Katriona after Catreen?"

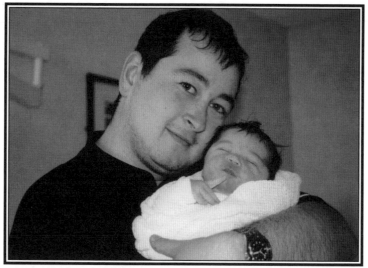

Robin Jr. and Katriona an hour after she entered the world.

Tears were rolling down faces on both sides of the Irish sea. We had been given a Katriona at last, 30 years after the first one. Two years later came Autumn Mary, our third grandchild. Now God started to birth something new in Robin and Emma. They both felt the time had come to move on. They were not sure where at first but they started to give away their furniture. God was telling them to start letting go.

Robin's heart was still for Canada. Emma now felt this was right too, so he started applying for full time Pastoral work. He was interested in leading worship, video and sound technology. Three churches were interested, then God brought about circumstances that made them consider a fourth. Emma's sister and her husband had started a work in Africa many years before. They have built a school and have a feeding programme which God has blessed. When they come home on deputation, Emma's mum Maureen goes out and looks after things. While she was there she made friends with a lovely christian girl Charlene, who was with Y.W.A.M. Charlene was from Canada and Maureen told her about Emma and Robin feeling God calling them to Canada. Charlene, who was a senior Pastor's daughter, said that their church was looking for a Worship

Pastor. Weeks of interviews by phone followed Robin's initial inquiry. Then the church flew Robin and Emma out to let them see the place and get to know them. They were offered the job.

It was not an easy decision to make. Leaving family and friends comes with a high price tag. They sold or gave away the last of their possessions. It was time to move on to the next chapter that God had prepared for them. With five suitcases, 3 children aged 2, 4 and 6 they boarded a plane, saying good bye to all that was familiar and trusted the God that they loved for their future in a new land. We too had to trust God with our children and grandchildren. We prayed that their new church family would love them and care for them for us. They have, and we are very grateful.

Robin, Emma and family have settled into their new country well. They have adjusted to very cold winters and very hot summers. There have been days of home sickness and all that entails. Making new friends and building up a home again, all take time. They moved a few weeks before Christmas and the church folk were wonderful. People gave them furniture and filled stockings for the children for Christmas as they could not fit many toys into their suitcases. They loved them in very practical ways.

Robin was able to realise part of his dream as he has a pilot permit license now and flies whenever he can. Some years ago when I reminded him about going into Christian work and not wanting to be a missionary or a Pastor he said,

"I didn't have a chance did I?"

I smiled, remembering once more that time when God had come near as I had prayed Hannah's prayer.

When Hannah took Samuel to the temple and left him there, the Bible says that she came back to see him every year and brought him a coat. I have asked the Lord that I might be able to see my son every year. So far, I have been able to do that. I don't bring him a coat, I bring what he asks for - Bisto granules and Cadbury's chocolate!

Chapter 34 🐦

CANADIAN ADVENTURE

When our son Robin and family moved to Edmonton, it became one of our goals to visit them. We wanted to meet their new church family and see a bit of the surrounding area. I looked at the map and all of a sudden had, what I thought, was a great idea. We would fly to Vancouver, hire a car, drive through the Rockies and visit some friends along the way. When I looked at it on the map it didn't seem too far at all if we had plenty of stops. So our plans were made for June 2006. It was a journey to remember and talk about to this day.

We were met by Jackie and Norah Murphy and their daughter Irene at the airport and how lovely it was to arrive at an airport and be welcomed. I had not seen any of them for 35 years. Norah and Jackie were the ones who had invited me to their church and home as a young girl of 12. They were instrumental in my coming to know the Lord. I spent many happy weekends at their home with Irene their daughter who was my age. We all recognized each other, shared memories and meals and had an evening at Irene and Don's home. It was

Granddaughters Autumn Mary and Katriona.

Grandson Torben.

lovely to be staying with Jackie and Norah again after all those years. The years disappeared as we laughed and shared each other's stories. They took us to see some sights and then brought us to the car hire showroom to collect our car for the rest of our journey. We had been blessed by their generosity and love. Then we were on our own.

When we were choosing the car to meet our needs we chose a car big enough to take our luggage but not one that would be a lot bigger than our car at home. We booked in, were given the key to the car and told where it was. We couldn't find it so I went back in and asked where it was again. I was told the car that we had booked was not available so we had been upgraded. When I told Robin we laughed but when we saw this massive car, we wondered how we would manoeuvre it. It would have held the luggage of a small town. The journey began. We were going across the American border into Seattle, staying the night with the son of some friends, Eva and Ken Needham. We did not want to be so close to them and not spend an evening there. Paul and Leanne very kindly kept supper until very late for us - on the map it did not look far at all but in reality it was a long way. By the time we got to Seattle, Robin was starting to feel ill with all the driving. I thought everything would be fine after a night's rest.

Next day, after a beautiful breakfast, we said our goodbyes and headed back towards Canada again through the mountains. The scenery was breathtaking and we marvelled at the Rockies. The idea to take a break at small towns on the way was a good idea, except there were no small towns close enough - they all seemed hundreds of miles apart. As the day went on Robin's pain level rose so much that he said,

"You'll have to drive".

Panic.................I couldn't believe it! Here we were in a strange country with strange road signs, driving on a different side of the road in what was the equivalent of a small bus and Robin was saying I had to drive! My prayer life went up a gear at that point. Mostly it was three word prayers,

"God help me." "God protect me." "God guide me."

I am so glad that God hears three word prayers. I was scared. Robin had to lie in the back for parts of the journey so sometimes I lost my navigator. When we were coming into large towns like Calgary I would get him in beside me to help me find the right intersections. What an adventure it turned out to be. We stayed with various hosts at B&B's, starting out early each morning for the next leg of our trip. Kamloops, Canmore, Lake Louise, Kelowna, Calgary, Banff. We saw them all. We had little picnics at lakes and watched the eagles soar above us. We drove slowly on the mountain roads, passing mountain goats that wanted us to stop and say hello. We always hoped that we would see a bear.

Before leaving Ireland my friends had warned me about the bears, "If you see a bear, Lavinia, don't be trying to stroke it or poke your head out the car window offering sweets."

"If I see a bear," I had said, "I will probably get so excited I'll run over and kiss it."

I was joking of course. They thought that was very funny. Then on the day we were to arrive at Edmonton, we passed a place called Innisfail Wildlife Park. It was Robin who saw it and because we were tired after another long drive, we decided to go in for a little while to get a break from sitting. We looked at tigers and monkeys and decided to stop for refreshments before going to see the bears. One of the Park workers asked if we were going to see the bears performing. She told us there would be a performance in about an hour. Then she said,

"You can even have your photograph taken kissing a bear."

Don't tell me that God doesn't have a sense of humour! When I questioned her more I realized that this was a gift from God and I knew He had prepared this wee surprise just for me. I know that not every woman would want to be kissed by a bear, but this was a memory that I knew would last a lifetime.

We watched the bears perform. They were amazing. These were movie star bears. They had been in lots of movies - Dr Doolittle 2, Grizzly Falls, The Last Trapper and Wild America. They'd also been used in TV commercials. Their trainer was called Ruth LeBarge. Most of the bears she had reared from cubs. Then came the question that I had been waiting for,

Lavinia kissed by a Grizzly.

"Would anyone like to have their photo taken with the bears?"

Grown men turned white and moved back - I ran forward and was first into the enclosure with the trainer and the bear. His name was Ali Oop, a 1400lb Grizzly. He had the most beautiful face.

I was told to stand with my arms behind my back and lean my head forward to him. I did what I was told and Ali Oop bent forward to my upturned face. You have no idea how big these bears are until you are up so close. His nose was almost the size of my face. He turned his big head from side to side, then he gave me a big kiss.........he actually gave me three. The trainer said,

"He likes you."

I still can't believe it sometimes. I was kissed by a Grizzly. However, I have the photo to prove it and Robin also took a video. It was worth that long scary drive for that experience.

An hour later we were with our family. This is what the journey was all about. This is why we came. All the other things were a bonus.

Our son sent copies of the picture home on the internet to my friends. "Mother tamed the bears in the Rockies," he wrote. They of course thought it was a set up until I came home and showed them the evidence!

Chapter 35 ✎

JESUS SAVIOUR PILOT ME

God gave me lots of gifts that holiday. Just being with the family was wonderful - the gift of joy that comes when you get to be Granny and Grandad for a while.

Then there was the gift of peace that came when we met the Pastors and leadership of the church where our son had become Pastor of Worship and Creative Arts - Godly, mature men who would look after our children. It was important for us to see that. They had left parents, grandparents, a great church and friends to start a new life in a country where they did not know anyone. When their blood family could not be there, they were embraced by a church family who showed them love and opened their hearts and homes to them.

I was asked to speak at a Ladies' event at the church while I was there. The evening had been very well thought through, much prayer and thoughtfulness showed in every detail from the worship to the decor of the hall. It was a joy to be part of such a lovely evening. After I spoke I had the chance to get to know some of the ladies. As we shared our lives and hearts

Speaking at Calvary Community Church, Edmonton.

with each other some lovely friendships were born - another gift from God. However, I received an unexpected gift right at the beginning of our holiday.

On the way to our son's home I saw a church notice board announcing there was to be a special concert. Janet Paschal was to be the singer. I could hardly believe it - Janet is one of my favourite singers. I got to know her songs through the Gaither videos. I then got to know a bit about her when I looked up her website and read her blog. Janet had been through a lot in the previous year with a diagnosis of Breast Cancer and the months of treatment that followed. I had never spoken to her personally but I had spoken to God about her a lot. Now, here she was on the road again and coming to a church that was just a few blocks away from where we were staying.

I knew from the minute I saw the notice that I had to be there. I did not know that it would be a significant night in my life. I am glad that God knows my needs and on this occasion even organized for me to cross an ocean to be where He could meet them. His timing is perfect. The following day I said to my daughter-in-law,

"Emma, there is a concert tomorrow night in a church not far from here. I feel I should go to it, will you come with me?"

"Yes I'll come with you Lavinia," she said.

The night of the concert I rushed the poor girl off her feet so that we could go early and get a good seat. We arrived and found seats and waited for the concert to begin. When I looked around, the church was not as crowded as I thought it would be. I later found out that something else was happening that night - Edmonton's Ice Hockey team, the Oilers, had made it through to the finals of the Stanley Cup. This was a great achievement and lots of people all over Edmonton and beyond stayed at home and watched the game, which was televised live.

When the concert started, Janet shared a bit about her journey over the past months and how she had wanted, when she was well enough, to go on tour and thank the people who had prayed for her personally. Edmonton was part of her tour. She had no way of knowing that there was a woman from Ireland there who had prayed for her too. As I sat listening, a sense of peace came over me and I could feel the presence of God in a special way. It was as if everyone else in the church disappeared and there was just me and God.

As a Christian speaker in Northern Ireland, it had been a busy few years - my diary had been full. I spoke at least 2 nights a week, sometimes travelling many miles to reach the Church or Prayer Breakfast at which I was to speak. I love what I do and I am so thankful to the Lord for letting me share my story and His love wherever I am invited. It's just that, when you are constantly giving out, you come to a place where you desperately need to receive. I was at that place. I was heart hungry for God. We all need to spend time in prayer and God's Word on a regular basis - that is something that should be part of our everyday lives but this feeling is different, when God uses someone else to speak into our lives, encouraging us, challenging us, renewing our vision, filling us with hope and the certainty that whatever happens, our God is able to bring us through. I felt all those things that night. As Janet quoted

Psalm 139, one of my favourite Psalms, I was reminded again that I can never be away from God's presence. He is everywhere and in everything. This mighty God knows me completely, even my very thoughts. Nothing is hidden from Him. My only response can be to say,

"Search me Oh God, and know my heart, test me and know my anxious thoughts.

See is there is any offensive way in me and lead me in the way everlasting."

As Janet sang "Jesus Saviour Pilot me over life's tempestuous sea," I was reminded that no matter how hard the journey would be, or how boisterous the angry waves that would lash my shore, He would always be there too. He is the compass and the guide. He has charted my course. When the storms come, and they do to us all, He whispers,

"Peace be still," into my tired and weary heart.

I came back to Ireland a different woman. I had received so much. People in Edmonton remember June 19th 2006, as the night the Oilers played in the Stanley Cup finals. I remember June 19th 2006, as the night I had an encounter with God that will have eternal significance, because all of our encounters with God do. What I find amazing is God's timing. He took me nearly four thousand miles for this encounter. He used someone that I had been praying for over the past year. He arranged both of our schedules for it to happen.

Thank you God.

Thank you Janet.

✎

Chapter 36 ❧

PAUL OPENS THE DOOR

Paul walked out of the school gates for the last time when he was sixteen. It was one of the happiest days of his life. He turned around, looked at the building and smiling said, "You'll never see me again."

Our second son had never enjoyed school. I remember when he was five years old and in his first year of school, a doctor came in to give the class a routine examination. The doctor chatted away to Paul and said,

"Do you like school?"

Paul thought for a minute and then replied,

"I like bits of it."

"What bits do you like?" the doctor asked.

"Break time and dinner time," was Paul's answer!

He never ever got to like the bits in between break time and dinner time. Years later we found out that he was dyslexic and this was the reason that he found school and concentration difficult. People with dyslexia lose concentration quickly and if they are not taught in a certain way lose interest in what is being said. They seem to switch off when they can't listen anymore. I think that I have a mild form of it myself. Yet Paul has knowledge that could never be found in a text book, an innate wisdom of things that cannot be taught. Because of these special gifts, he is an incredibly caring man.

He has always been drawn to those who are hurting or lonely. He sees the pain in people's eyes that most of us miss. Paul did not like competitive games because he knew winning meant someone had to lose. He likes to make others happy and goes out of his way to do that. People are comfortable being with him because he has a great gift of encouragement and he makes others feel good about themselves.

Not long after leaving school, Paul went into the work of Sandes. Soon he was bringing the soldiers home for meals, taking them out to church or hanging around the Sandes Centre, just listening to other young men pour out their troubles. Mark Farmer, the Superintendent gave Paul permission to keep the Centre open as long as he liked. Mark and Paul had a great working relationship and Paul benefited greatly from Mark's wisdom and encouragement. They both had the same vision for the work and it was not long until the building was filled with young soldiers and youth from the church fellowship. Paul would bring the guitar and they would sing and chat into the small hours.

Music has been a big part of Paul's life. His love of words gave him the ability to write the lyrics of some great songs. One song that he wrote was called 25 Years and was played constantly on the radio. He was the lead singer in a band and they played many venues throughout Northern Ireland.

A different band to "The Persuaders", their vision was for the pubs and clubs, bringing positive lyrics into a sometimes dark music scene.

One night Paul was leading worship at the church youth fellowship when a young girl turned up whom he had not seen before. She had an abundance of beautiful auburn hair and green eyes.

Her name was Julia and she had just returned from Stirling University where she had received a BA Honours in Economics. She had been asked to speak that night on what it was like being a Christian at University. I asked Julia to tell me about their meeting.

Julia said that she asked someone about Paul and was told that he worked for a Christian organization called Sandes in Ballykinler Barracks. That night he had a few soldiers with him and she thought that he had to be a special sort of person to do that work. As they spoke afterwards she thought he was funny and cheeky and she liked that. The weeks went on and Paul started to phone Julia. They became friends and Julia realized that she had feelings for Paul that she had not had for anyone else. The thing that worried her was the age difference. He was 18 and she was 23. However, they started going out together and soon they fell in love. After a few years I gained another beautiful daughter-in-law. They have been married 10 years and have one of the happiest marriages that I have ever seen.

They were not married long when one night Paul came home from work without his socks and shoes. When Julia questioned him about it, he told her the story. That day he had come across an old man who lived rough. The man had only one boot on because some children had run off with the other one. Paul chatted to him for a while, then seeing his feet were similar in size, took off his socks and shoes and gave them to him. Julia was glad he had given his shoes away. To them that was the normal thing to do. They have given themselves away to others over the years in many ways.

In 2003 Paul and Julia went to work in America. They became foster parents for an organization which ran a programme for troubled teenagers. They fell in love with New England where they had been sent and, when they came home after 18 months, longed to be back again. It is not an easy thing to emigrate to America. There was only one way that they might have a chance. A scheme called the Green Card Lottery. You make an application and an electronically generated computer randomly selects names to be admitted. Providing the interview is passed, you get a Green Card which allows you to work and live in America. America takes in 55,000 people a year this way, which seems a lot but considering 13.5 million apply, the chances are quite low. Some people have tried all their lives

Paul and Julia in Maine.

Paul with Fergus and Barrett in New England.

and have never been chosen. Paul and Julia were accepted the first year they entered - they had followed their hearts and God had opened the door.

They went back to the same job but have just recently had a change of careers. Julia is at present working with homeless young people in a drop in centre. She is also studying at the University of Southern Maine, working towards a Masters degree in Counselling Education which will qualify her to be a Licensed Clinical Professional Counsellor. Paul really wanted to work for the Sheriff's Department but there was only one problem - an entry exam! Paul applied and Julia worked with him helping him with study methods that he could understand. He passed the exam first time as well as all the interviews that followed. The next hurdle was the training. Four weeks were academic with an exam every morning. Once again Julia helped with revision, we prayed and Paul passed every one of them. Not only did he pass, he graduated first in his class. We all cried tears of joy that day. When God wants us somewhere, nothing can stop it and as always, He is an abundant God.

Paul and Julia live in a beautiful part of Maine - their house is beside a lake. They have their own dock and they kayak whenever they can, watching the bald eagles flying overhead and listening to the cry of the loons. They both run a few miles every day with their dogs Barrett and Fergus. They love their new country and have settled well. They too have known the pain of good-byes as they left behind great friends and loving families. We miss them very much but because we love them, we let them go with God's blessing, and who would have thought that it would be this son who would bring about a dream that God had placed in my heart before he was even born.

Chapter 37 🐦

AMERICAN DREAM

You will know when God plants a dream in your heart. You will know by its persistence. It's a different feeling to just hoping that something will happen. When God plants a dream in your heart it will not go away. There may be circumstances that bury it for a while, but it will not die. It will come back again as strongly as it ever was before, because when God plants a dream it takes root and from that little seed it grows into what it will become. Often when you think your dream will never happen - it does so in a way you could never have imagined.

The dream was planted in my heart in July 1973. It's recorded in the chapter 'On The Road'. That day when the Pastor from America asked if we would come and sing at his church - that's when it happened. I was hoping to go the next week - that's the way I am! The others were more realistic and it seemed that I was the only one who caught the vision.

The years passed. Life happened, as life does. The children were born and their feet grew quicker than our bank balance so we had to buy them shoes. After ten years I said,"Lord, what about America?"

Twenty years passed.

"Lord, what about America?" I asked again.

I could not get the feeling out of my heart that America was going to be part of my life and not as a holiday but as was asked by that Pastor. There was singing involved and possibly speaking. When it got to twenty five years I started to send away for brochures. I felt it was coming soon. I was particularly drawn to New England. I got the literature and for the next five years read all I could about it. Robin would shake his head, laugh and say,

"Why are you getting those brochures? There's no chance we will be going there."

There were times when I almost believed him, but the dream would not go away. Then one day thirty years after the seed was planted, something happened that was to bring it about.

Our son Paul and his wife Julia came for Sunday dinner. As I was putting out the dinner I noticed they were both looking a bit strange, then Paul said,

"Julia and I have been looking at the possibility of working abroad again."

I was worried then because they had spent some time working in an orphanage in South Africa and had not stayed as long as they thought they would. They loved the work but the troubled land and danger they faced was too much of a reminder of our own situation and unrest in Northern Ireland at the time. I never thought they would think about leaving again.

I asked the question, almost afraid of hearing the answer.

"Where are you thinking of going?"

"America," Paul said.

As soon as he said it I felt a thump in my chest almost like my heart expanding in a beat.

"What part of America?"

"Some place called Maine in New England," Paul answered.

I knew that they would get the job. This was it. Deep in my heart I could feel that at last my dream would become reality.

"You'll get the job," I said.

"We haven't even applied yet, how do you know?" Julia said.

I told them the story about that day at Scrabo Tower and how I had felt ever since.

As we talked during dinner they told us the job was to be House Parents. They would be fostering some teenagers and living in a home that the organization would provide. They would be able to live and work in America for 18 months. They did not know where Maine was so I got out my brochures and maps and showed them the area that they were talking about.

"How come you have got these?" Julia asked.

"I've been waiting to go for a long time," I said.

Paul and Julia got the job and moved to America. It was exactly thirty years after that day at Scrabo Tower when I went to America for the first time. Looking back I wonder what my reaction would have been all those years ago, if I had been told it would happen through a child who was not going to be born for another four years and then I would have to wait until he became a man. How glad I am that God knows what is best and that His timing is perfect. Paul and Julia did not have their own home when we went out the first few times and so I looked up cottages to rent on the internet. I found what I was looking for in a little place called Fayette. I was drawn to it because its pasture backed on to a Baptist Church.

As I communicated with the owners, it became apparent that God had directed me to this place. Arn and Leda Sturtevant loved the Lord and we were amazed that God had brought us all together. Robin and I were asked to sing at Fayette Baptist Church and I was asked to share my story. This was how the dream had started all those years ago. It was a special day and as I went unto the platform to speak, I realized that it had happened at last. God's timing was perfect for many reasons. As I shared with the people that morning I knew that thirty years earlier I would not have had the same story to tell of the Lord's faithfulness and what He had brought me through. God had done a lot in me during those thirty years.

Lavinia and Robin singing in Fayette Baptist Church, USA.

Robin and Lavinia at at Arn and Leda's cottage by the lake.

*Gwen, Arn, Crawford, Leda and Robin - a second day at Arn and Leda's
cottage. As Arn prayed there was such a sweet sense of God's presence I
moved out of the circle and took this shot. Moments like this are not often
captured. This picture tells its own story.*

We have been back many times since then. America has
been like a present. Each time I unwrap a layer I find something
beautiful underneath. We have made many friends and thank
the Lord for the way He has led us each time we go there. In the
great scheme of things, my dream was very simple. People
have all sorts of dreams, like climbing to the top of Everest or
winning a gold medal in the Olympics. Some dream of finding
cures for terrible diseases and others dream about changing the
world through politics. Those dreams were not made for me but
my dream was and I loved having my dream and walking into
it when the time was right.

In his book 'The Dream Giver', Bruce Wilkinson says,
"Your dream is somewhere waiting for you. And if you don't
pursue it, something very important won't happen."

When God gives us a dream, it is not just for ourselves, it
is part of a plan for others as well. In God's time scale those
thirty years were necessary for us to meet the people that He

wanted us to meet and to share our lives with now. People that needed us to minister to them.

We have rejoiced with them over the years and we have grieved with them too. As they have opened their homes and hearts to us, we do the same for them. Some of them had a dream. That dream was to come to Ireland. As I open the door of our little cottage and welcome them in, my heart almost bursts with the joy of it. God's plan was much bigger than I could ever have imagined, because it was written in Heaven a long, long time ago.

Chapter 38 ❦

ON THE ROAD SECOND TIME AROUND

The checklist before going out to speak is a lot different second time around. As a young woman with the singing group, "The Persuaders", it was making sure we had a list of songs and the song book. The guitars were tuned and we packed all the various wires and speakers for our P.A. System. Maisie and I usually threw in a can of hair spray to tame the styles of the 70's and were even known to keep a few rollers in until we were nearly at our destination.

Whenever the babies came along we added bottles and nappies to our equipment. These were the days before disposable nappies so our bags were always full. As babies need to be entertained and don't always sleep on journeys, we often had to remind each other to take the rollers out before arriving at the church. Looking back I wonder where we got the energy, as most of us got up for work the next day and were often out singing and speaking five nights a week.

So, what does the checklist look like now for me? A bag large enough to carry a notebook, my glasses, a bottle of water, directions, painkillers, a road map and my Bible. On a good night I get into my car with all of these things but most times my husband comes out after me carrying the notebook or the glasses. He knows to look around when I head for the car because I often forget something.

When the boys were up and more independent I started to take speaking engagements and for many years now, I have spoken in Northern Ireland once or twice a week. I have learnt how to read a map the right way round, follow road numbers and know approximately how long it will take me to get to my destination. I have travelled alone for almost all of my journeys and am amazed at how I have found churches without the help of a sat nav, since when I go into a room with two doors, I don't know which one to go out again! I have even been known to get lost in friends' houses. Yet, this is the one God chooses to send out up country roads, to the back of beyond in the middle of winter. Even without the aforementioned hopeless sense of direction, it is almost impossible on a dark night, in the rain, to drive, read directions and follow road signs. Yet it happens and every week I get the opportunity to find out once again, that God's grace is sufficient.

I love how the Living Bible puts it in 2 Corinthians 12 v 9. "My power shows up best in weak people." God knows my weaknesses, but I have known His power. Can I just encourage you to trust God if He is asking you to do something that you feel you can't do? That's what faith is - trusting when you don't know the outcome, believing for things you cannot see. Journeys into the unknown are never easy but with each step your faith will grow. You will get to the stage where you realize that you can't - but He can.

I have loved travelling and sharing my faith with so many people. I share what the Lord has shown me, often through funny stories because I have learnt to laugh at myself, and also from life, because life teaches us many things. I also love the Word of God. As I read the gospels, I see Jesus telling stories about things of everyday life, like lost coins and lost sheep, bread that doesn't rise, prodigals - all things that people could identify with. Our God does not change and still cares about the things that are part of all our lives. I see this loving God pursuing people because of His deep love and commitment to them. I see a Shepherd who searches for lost sheep down dark streets with feet that bleed. I see Him lift that lost sheep and carry it on His shoulders. I see Him enter into the darkness of a broken mind and whisper, "all will be well". I see Him everywhere and in everything. I have been privileged to share what He has shown to me and I am so grateful that He has trusted me enough to let me do this. I am not qualified, but He is.

As I have travelled all over Northern Ireland and beyond, there is one thing that I have missed - the fellowship that I had when we sang as a group. I have missed talking and praying together before a meeting and the company on the long drive home. Life on the road can be lonely. So, as I am fast approaching sixty, I have wondered how much longer I should take bookings. Then just as I was about to buy a pair of slippers and settle down, the Lord surprised me again.

Maisie and I have remained friends. Ours has always been a special relationship. We have a deep respect for each other and a simple but strong faith that has never wavered. Our years on the road singing laid a foundation for many other years of service in the Lord's work. We have taught Sunday School, been officers in the Girls Brigade, spoken at meetings, led worship and sang with others over the years since I moved out of Belfast. Yet over and over again, God brings us back together.

We have both had busy lives. Looking after our families, working and church often meant that contact was limited to a few phone calls a year. It did not matter - our friendship was such that we never made demands on each other, just were delighted when it was possible to meet or even have a chat on the phone. During those chats we would often talk about those days out singing and how the Lord had blessed us, remembering the sweet sense of God's presence, thankful in our hearts for those years. I remember one of us saying on one occasion, "Wouldn't you give anything to have a night of it again?"

We don't have the energy that those young girls had but our hearts have not changed at all. One of the songs we sang

The song goes on - Lavinia and Maisie singing again.

At Dunmurry Church of God.

At Bangor Elim.

was called "Through it all". It talked about sorrows and God being there, trust when there was no understanding and strength through trials. We have both known all of those things in our lives, we have also lived long enough to know that every word that we sang was true because through it all we have known the Lord's faithfulness, we have never had to face one trial alone. He has said in His Word that He will never leave us or forsake us and He keeps His word. We have proved it to be true.

Our families have grown up now and we are at a different stage of our lives. I am often asked when I go out to speak if I would sing a song. I asked Maisie if she would like to come out with me sometimes and sing. She said, "I'd love to." God must have taken seriously those conversations that we had because here we are, second time around thirty five years after the first time and it's as if we have never stopped. As we sing, a sweet sense of God's presence falls around us like a cloak. She looks at me with tear filled eyes and says,

"It's like ointment, isn't it?"

"Yes, it's like ointment," I reply.

..........I'll not bother buying the slippers for a while!

Chapter 39 ❧

TERRIBLE PAWS

For those who know me this chapter will not be a surprise. For those who don't it's confession time. I have two great weaknesses. I've got more than that really but these are the two I am willing to talk about. The first one is chocolate. My motto has always been "a bar of chocolate a day, keeps the long face away". For me any brand of chocolate will do, I am not a fussy woman. If I was ever elected into Parliament I would pass a law that everyone should eat a bar of chocolate a day. I am convinced this would bring about world peace!

The second weakness is cats - those beautiful furry creatures with whiskers, a leg on every corner and a tail. They fascinate me. Since having my first cat Darkie (this is the same Darkie that travelled to England in a suitcase) I've always had at least one in the house, although I've never owned one because you can't own a cat - they own you and train you very quickly. If one ever jumps on to your knee and purrs then you feel that a great honour has been bestowed on you and you get a warm happy feeling inside, at least I do. I am told this does not happen to people who do not like cats. The following story shows that God has a sense of humour, and when He wants to tell us something He will use whatever is necessary to make us listen.

The months of June ,July and August are months when I do not have many speaking engagements and I use them as a time to seek the Lord for the following church year. Usually the Lord will give me a verse of scripture and I will know that this will be the verse that I need to think about for the following year. It's a verse I hold on to and the Lord shows me different treasures over the months as I use this verse in different ways.

A few years ago when I asked the Lord for a word I got a very strange answer. I heard these words very clearly in my mind,

"Terrible paws if he didn't know how to velvet them."

Now I am not a theologian but I knew that, although I recognised these words, they were not scripture. I could not think where I had heard them before. After a few days I typed them into the computer, and found they were from a book called The Lion ,The Witch and The Wardrobe by C.S.Lewis. One of the children in the story Lucy, on seeing the size of the lion Aslan's paws thinks,

"Terrible paws if he didn't know how to velvet them".

All very well I thought, but I wanted a scripture. Surely the Lord did not want me to speak about paws.

Some weeks passed and I started to think it was the devil keeping those words coming into my mind. Then I got a phone call from an animal shelter asking if I would foster a kitten as the shelter was full up. I said, "certainly", and a lady called with a tiny kitten not more than 6 weeks old. The poor little thing had been found abandoned, injured and afraid. I looked into the carrier at this little scrap sitting there. She looked like she was smiling because her bottom lip was cut and it had carved a smile into her face.

She did not draw back when I spoke to her but raised her paw straight up and held it there as if to say "Hi".

I thought, "Lord you've sent me a charismatic kitten. I've never had one of those before!"

By this time my big Maine Coon cat, who is 20lbs of fur and muscle, was pushing his head against the cage. His head was bigger than all of the kitten. He made it clear that he wanted her out. He cried in at her and she looked at him as if she had found her lost mother again. I took a risk, opened the cage, and watched carefully. What happened next was amazing. She walked straight to him. He walked around her then lay down, put his big paw out and pulled her close and washed her little face. When I saw the way he held on to her with his paws, a light came on. I was seeing those words that had kept running around in my head. This was it. Those big paws could really have caused a lot of damage, but he recognized that she was injured, lost and afraid. He knew she needed help.

It will not surprise you to learn that my cat's name is Aslan. At cat shows people say he is like a lion. This massive Red Tabby lives up to his name. As for me, sometimes slow to listen and hear what God is saying, I am just thankful that He brought about a situation to bring those words to life.

Aslan and Willow, best friends.

Aslan looking after Willow.

I said "Yes Lord, teach me what you want me to say through what I see."

I watched and learnt that summer. I watched as she snuggled into him when she was tired. I watched when she looked for him if he left her alone for a while. I watched his patience as she jumped on him, often landing straight on his face. She followed him everywhere. He washed her for Ireland - there never was a cleaner kitten. He taught her how to use the cat flap. He taught her how to read the clock and if feed time was one minute later than usual, she wailed. He taught her to listen carefully for any tin being opened because it usually meant a meal was on its way. I watched as he gently licked her sore swollen lip until it was better again. But mostly it was those big paws I watched. When he needed to rest and she kept biting his ears, or pulling his tail, he would pull her in close pushing her down gently but firmly with his big paw, letting her know that she had gone far enough.

Willow gets her morning wash..

She seemed to know he was serious when he did this and settled down curling up close to his chest and falling asleep in his paws. I watched hundreds of sermons played before my eyes that summer and shared them the following church year with those words that I had almost ignored.

"Terrible paws if he did not know how to velvet them."

P.S. She is two years old now. Her name is Willow. We felt we could not separate them because the bond between them was special. He still washes her in the mornings while she looks at him with a funny look that says, "I can wash myself, I am a big girl now."

Aslan is still winning cat shows and is a Grand Premier (champion) now. He certainly deserves a prize for fostering Willow and for teaching me about the love and Fatherhood of God.

Chapter 40 ❧

LOVED WITH EVERLASTING LOVE

As I look back over the years that the Lord has given me, there are two things that have always amazed me - God's unconditional love and God's provision. My life has been filled with both. When God came into my life I had nothing to offer, only my brokenness and pain, but He said, "I love you just the way you are."

I have known His love from that moment on. I have also been stretched beyond what I am capable of, sometimes resulting in things that now make me laugh as I look back and remember.

Not having been brought up to attend Sunday School and church, my Bible knowledge was not wonderful. However, I loved God's Word and would read it whenever I could. One night, as part of the group The Persuaders, we went to sing at a church, only to realize that they wanted us to take the whole service, including the sermon. I asked Robin and Sammy if one of them would speak but they were horrified. I knew not to ask Maisie - she would have collapsed. The three of them looked at me and said, "You speak, you can speak."

I could speak, but I did not know what I was speaking about. That did not bother them as long as they did not have to do it.

When this sort of thing happens it is good for your prayer life. I said, "God help me."

I am good at three word prayers!

I thought about the story that I had read in the Bible that morning and knew that I could share that.

At that stage of my journey I was reading from the King James version of the Bible. I had read that morning about Zacchaeus. The Bible says that he was 'The Chief Publican'.

Relating the story, I told the congregation, "Not only did this man own a pub, he owned the biggest pub in town."

The only publicans I knew were the ones on our street corners. The people were laughing and I thought they were really enjoying the sermon.

Robin told me afterwards, that in the Bible the word publican meant 'tax collector'. I was so upset - I had just taken it as I had read it. I remember saying to Robin that night that I would never speak again because I was teaching the people lies. He knew better and the following day, he went into town and bought me a copy of "The Living Bible" and here I am 38 years later, still speaking and using that story to let people see that if God can use someone who did not know what a publican was, what could He do with someone who did?

Such is the love of God that not only does He take us just the way we are, He does not give up on us when we get it wrong…….. especially when we get it wrong. He is not ashamed of who we are because He sees past our lack of ability and sees our hearts. Years ago when I was a young girl, I remember my Pastor saying,

"God is not looking for your ability, He is looking for your availability."

He has poured His mercy over my life, and even when my heart has deceived me, He has been there again and again with abundant grace.

He takes people who can't and turns them into people who can, because He chooses to reveal His power. He did it with

Moses and Gideon. Moses did not have the words, Gideon did not have the courage. God saw past those things and they found the words and the courage and changed history. God is bigger than our background. I have known His unconditional love poured over my life like ointment bringing healing and peace.

Then there is God's provision. I could write a whole book on this one subject. I have never had to worry about my needs being met because my Father knows my needs before I ask. I also believe that we all can be part of God's plan to meet the needs of others, in whatever way God has made it possible for us to do that. We can all give some part of ourselves away. One of the things that God has asked me to do over the years, is to give people my time. He still asks this of me.

God has supplied our needs in many ways. He has used people who love us to give us gifts. He has used unconventional methods that have made us laugh and He has gifted me with creativity to make and sell all sorts of crafts. It has been challenging at times. Coming out of the work of Sandes in our forties and starting again without the wedding presents was not easy. When we moved into the camp we had given most of our things away. So we started again, cutlery, kettles, the lot. Then when we had just got our house together, Robin took ill and had to leave work long before we ever expected. This was without a doubt, another challenge.

There is however, another side to all of this - it is also an adventure. Part of me enjoys sitting back and watching God do the miracles time after time. I have never had to worry about God meeting our needs, the question is how He will do it? Our God is full of surprises, He is Jehovah Jireh. His ways are sometimes very funny and Robin and I have laughed over the years at the methods that our Great God has used, as illustrated in the following story.

In order to get a good price for the flights over to see our boys, I need to book quite early. A few years ago I was really struggling to do this. I was £200 short and time was ticking by. Then we received a letter from someone who just felt they should send us a gift. It was £100. The following week our cat

Big grumpy cat!

Aslan was entered in a cat show. There are three cat shows in Northern Ireland every year and he is entered in them all. The day of the show he got car sick and was in terrible form. By the time we got to the venue he had definitely got a grumpy head on! He protested every time a judge lifted him out to assess him and one judge could not get him out of his cage at all. Aslan is

Aslan wins the show!

a Maine Coone, he weighs 20lbs and these are not easy cats to pull about if they decide they don't want to move. We thought that was that - he would not be taking home a rosette that day. We hadn't thought there would be a miracle that day. As the show went on, Aslan kept getting 1st in all his important classes. He beat cats from all over Ireland, Scotland and England to be best of all the Semi long haired cats in the show. Then he was up against all the other Best of Breeds in their sections. Aslan went on to win the whole show. I can only assume his good looks and grooming spoke louder than his manners that day.

Normally the winning cat will receive a supply of cat food and a bed, or litter and a trophy. This time it was a money prize. I have never been in a show that had one before, or since. Aslan won the prize. I am sure you can guess how much it was - £100.

As Robin and I carried the big grumpy cat out of the show that day all we could do was smile. I said, "God, you've done it again."

This time He even used the cat to help us!

We would get to see our boys.

Chapter 41 ❧

RESTORATION

My husband tells people who visit us not to stand in one place too long or there is a chance that they will get painted or have a piece of lace added to them. He says this because I love restoring things. I love to get into a junk shop. I find old stuff that nobody wants and I sand it, prime it and repaint it. I then add an antiquing wax. I love taking something that has been thrown aside and making it into something useful, maybe even changing it from what it was originally intended for. I can see past age, varnish and neglect. I see what it can become with a bit of work.

I like to make things with material too, little cushions and hanging bags with "sayings " on them. I cover things in lace and would never ever throw away a button because someday the perfect place will turn up for that button. There is no doubt, I am a Magpie. I have even made a cover for my upright hoover. A bear with a long flowing dress stands in my bathroom, and you would never guess that it housed a hoover underneath. My friend Gloria laughs at my hoover cover. I don't know why - I think it's cute. She lives in fear that I will make her one for a present someday!

This is who I am, this is the way God made me. If I am not making something or restoring something, after a while I don't feel right at all, hardly knowing what to do with myself. As a young girl with no bedside cabinet, our local fruit shop gave me an orange crate. I wallpapered it with pink and white striped paper and it looked great as a book case. Back then, that was a necessity because we did not have much. Now, it is a choice.

I have been recycling long before it became the "in thing". I have no desire to buy new - I love old, worn and battered,

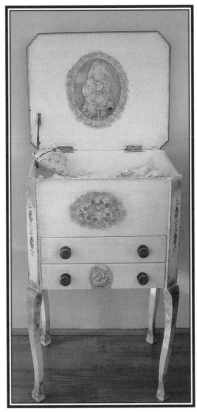

The old restored sewing cabinet.

things like my sewing cabinet, an old battered mahogany piece with two drawers and a lift up lid. However, it had beautifully shaped legs. I got it for £5 at a car boot sale. I sanded it and painted it a soft cream, put some pale green wax highlights on parts of the legs then finished it with some burnt umber paint, giving it an aged look. It has its original handles which I think are brass but I have left them as they are, almost black. Each time I look at it I smile.

As I sand and paint and wax what most people dispose of, there is not a time that I don't think of my Father. He is in the restoration business too. He specializes in putting people together again - taking the unlovely and making them beautiful, repairing the broken in body and mind. He picks up those who have been discarded or seen as useless and makes them into people of purpose and value. He washes away the dirt and grime that years of pain and despair have brought about. He adds lustre and sparkle where once dullness and apathy reigned. He lingers lovingly over those whose hearts have been broken and whose lives have fallen apart and He puts them together again. He sees the finished product, the potential that no-one else can see.

With patience, faithfulness and love, this great God comes into our lives and changes us from the inside out. He's the God of the second chance, the One who makes all things new. The One who says, "I will restore to you the years that the locusts have eaten."

We are a work in progress, because it takes time to be rebuilt. It doesn't happen all at once. When God touches and restores us, we are never the same again. Even the painful parts of our lives that have left scars can be used. With God nothing is wasted. He uses every part of us, even the pain. It's what makes us who we are. I could never have worked for 16 years with people who had lost their babies, if I had not lost four of my own. Those scars became a bridge to help others who were going through the pain and grief that the loss of a baby brings. And, although we may not like it, there is a growing that takes place in the painful times of our lives that brings a depth and knowledge to us that we could not have found any other way. We become more 'Real'.

One of my favourite books is called "The Velveteen Rabbit", by Margery Williams. It's a children's book but has a very special appeal for adults too. It's about toys in a child's nursery that come alive after dark. There is a conversation between the Velveteen Rabbit and an old Horse that describes this becoming 'Real' so very well. The Rabbit asks the Horse,"What is Real?"

This is the reply:

"Real isn't how you are made," said the Skin Horse. "It's a thing that happens to you. When a child loves you for a long, long time, not just to play with but really loves you, then you become real."

"Does it hurt?" asked the Rabbit.

"Sometimes," said the Skin Horse, for he was always truthful. "When you are Real you don't mind being hurt."

"Does it happen all at once, like being wound up," he asked, "or bit by bit?"

"It doesn't happen all at once," said the Skin Horse. "You become. It takes a long time. That's why it doesn't often happen to people who break easily, or who have been carefully kept. Generally, by the time you are Real, most of your hair has been loved off and your eyes drop out and you get loose in the joints and very shabby. But these things don't matter at all, because once you are Real you can't be ugly........once you are Real you can't become unreal again. It lasts for always."

Some of the most Real people I know are the ones who have been through pain and suffering. When they have come out the other side of sorrow and have taken on sometimes different roles in life than they had originally intended, they have been a blessing and an encouragement to many. Their lives say to others,

"You can make it, I did."

They "Become".

When God touches and rebuilds the broken they are never the same again. He has said in His Word,

"I will build you up again and you will be rebuilt."

It lasts for always.

❧

Chapter 42 ❧

MORE THAN ENOUGH

Robin and I love our little house in the country. We live quite close to Tyrella beach and although we can't see it, we can hear the roar of the waves whenever the tide is in. If we want to go down to walk by the sea, we just have to go down a lane not far from the house and about a 15 minute walk over the fields takes us there. Our part of the beach is usually empty. It is beautiful in all seasons. The curlews and the gulls talk in their own distinctive language and we love to hear their cries as we look out towards the sea and the beautiful Mountains of Mourne.

Over the years we had talked about an alternative lifestyle - one that meant we could spend more time walking on the beach, not slipping a few hours in at weekends, when all the other things were taken care of. There was something appealing about the solitude and the peace that comes from being at one with nature. Reality was a mortgage which we did not take out until our forties, two sons and three cats. Neither of us were born into money, so we tidied the dream up and tucked it away.

The years passed, the boys married, the cats died and were replaced by others. We had moved from the work in Sandes. Robin was a Project Manager for an Engineering firm. I was self-employed, making floral arrangements, crafts and painting ceramics. Life was busier than ever when one day something happened that was to change everything . It was the start of our alternative lifestyle. It happened in a way we could never have imagined and probably would not have signed up for if we had been given the choice.

It was just another busy day for me. I finished the ironing, packed the clothes into a suitcase as we were travelling the following day to visit our son and daughter-in-law in Kent. I put the ironing board away and as I was bending to put the iron in the cupboard something happened in my back. The searing pain shot down my leg and for a while I could not move in any direction. It was a few minutes before I could straighten myself. Even taking a breath was sore. I dragged my leg behind me and somehow got on top of the bed. I knew that whatever I had done was not going to go away quickly. However, I had no idea just how things would change because of it.

With the aid of painkillers, prayer and a hot water bottle on my back I got some sleep that night, but the journey the following day was agony. I was very sore after the flight and the drive from the airport to Kent. I convinced myself that I would be better in a few days. We tried to go out and about but when I sat down it was difficult getting up and when I was up it was worse getting down. I dragged my leg behind me, took more painkillers and only succeeded in making things worse.

A few days later my husband and son drove me into the hospital where I was carried in by two ambulance men as walking by now was impossible. A disc problem was diagnosed and I was given enough painkillers for the next few days and enough to see me home to Ireland. We had to buy an extra seat on the plane as I could not sit up but had to lie. I had never had pain like this before and my leg was numb down the inside. I was told to lie in bed for 3 weeks. That I could do. I lay on my right side because it was the only way to lie that did not cause pain.

I started to recover after the three weeks thanks to my husband, next door neighbour and also my dear friend Patricia who came to help with so many practical things that I could not do for myself. I sat up in bed, started to move around and the physiotherapist came to the house to help get me mobile again. Then one morning I sat up awkwardly in bed and started the whole thing over again. More lying in bed, more painkillers. My life was lived from a bed over the next months. After 4 months I was sent for a scan. I had to lie in the back of a friend's car for the journey. The scan said that everything was alright. I am convinced that the machine was not working that day as nobody could have this much pain and be alright. Gradually I got on my feet again. I was not able to drive for nearly a year. Everything was different. Everything had changed.

Where was God in all of this? He was there too in that pain-filled time. There were days when pain and loneliness clouded my vision. I was the one who ran instead of walking, my diary was always full and now I had to learn to live a life from my bed a good part of the time. It was not easy. It took a while for me to learn how to worship God outside of church. Since giving my life to Christ as a young girl of 12, church had been a big part of my life. There were never enough meetings for me to go to. Although I had always known God's presence with me in my everyday life there had always been something special to me, an excitement, when I walked into God's house. I loved worship, I loved sermons and listening to what God had to say through those who brought His Word, I also loved the fellowship. Now I had to learn to walk alone, to find God just where I was. I'd like to say that I got deeper into God's Word, that my prayer times were powerful but that did not happen. Pain killers dull the mind and my thinking was not always sharp. I did get to know a bit about me. Someone said in a sermon one time, "What we are under pressure is what we are."

I did not always like the person that I was at the beginning as I struggled with my different life style. I had to learn that when all the props were taken away, God was still there. I learned lessons that I could not have learned had I not been in the place where I could be still and alone. I never lost the feeling

Beach walk.

that God was close, because He never leaves us. I felt His love in that pain filled time and I found out that He is enough.

There will be times in all our lives when things happen that we can't change and the only thing left is for us to change. It is one of the hardest things to do. At first I just wanted things to be back the way they were before I hurt my back. Then I accepted that it couldn't be that way. I had to let a lot of things go. When I did that, God eventually opened other doors. Sometimes we hold on to things longer than God intends for us. We do them because we have always done them, or because people expect us to. Occasionally we even think that no-one can do them as well as we can and what we do is stop others having the opportunity to be part of God's plan.

My back never recovered completely and there are times when I have to go to bed for short periods. I rest a little, move a little, get on the painkillers as soon as I can and just know that unless God heals me this is going to be part of my life. As a speaker it is sometimes inconvenient as bookings are often taken a year in advance. I have on occasions had to phone and say "I am coming but I will need someone to help me to get out of the car when I get there." After the service they get me back into the car for going home and I toot the horn when I arrive back and my husband comes and gets me out again. As yet I have never had to cancel. When I travel out of Ireland I have a friend Gwen whom I jokingly call my minder, who comes with me. She is amazing - she lifts the cases and makes sure that I get there in one piece. She is also one of my prayer partners and looks after me spiritually too. I have had to learn to make myself vulnerable and ask for help whenever I need it.

Paul, Julia and Robin going down our lane that leads to the sea.

Life has seasons for us all. Change comes to each of our lives - sickness, death, divorce or redundancy. All bring their own sorrow and sometimes it feels as if we are drowning in a sea of pain. God has never promised that we would have a life free from trouble and pain but He has said that He will be with us in our pain. He is the only one who does not change and He is enough.

It is Enough!

When my dreams just fade away and slowly die,
When my eye glints not with joy but with a tear,
I turn my head to hear Love's far-off whisper,
And I know that God the Lord is drawing near.

When the song within my heart turns into silence,
When the stream of joy dries up without a trace,
Then I search to see the dawn of glory breaking,
And I catch a fleeting glimpse of Jesus' face.

When the structures of my faith begin to crumble,
When the pillars that I leaned on start to fall,
Then I dig deep once again to touch the bedrock
And on Jesus build a structure standing tall.

When all my precious things are taken from me,
And what is left seems worthless and so small,
Then I hear His voice and realise that I have Jesus,
It is enough! for He is All in All.

In Jesus I have dreams beyond compare,
A song of praise that soars to heaven above,
A faith that rests on Jesus, my foundation,
And all the glorious treasures of His love.

- Gloria Kearney

Chapter 43 ❧

ALTERNATIVE LIFESTYLE

Our alternative lifestyle was taking shape. The problem was it was taking a different shape to what we had in mind. I was living at a much slower pace. I had Gynae problems and a prolapsed womb brought the inevitable decision that a hysterectomy was the only answer. There was also a theory that it might be contributing to the back pain. So, I went off to have a Happy Hysterectomy!

I called it a Happy Hysterectomy because I was glad that the decision had finally been taken out of my hands. I have been meeting with my 3 prayer partners on Friday nights now for 12 years. On the Friday night before my operation we had a special night. We had a little celebration complete with cakes and buns and raised our glasses of Shloer to a Happy Hysterectomy.

I tell everyone that I had a double Hysterectomy, because like a lot of things in my life, it did not go the way I thought it would. I was brought back to the ward and was just coming round from the anaesthetic when I was told I was going back to theatre as there was a problem. Another anaesthetic. All the stitching that had been so carefully completed, was unpicked again as they went inside to find out what was causing me to bleed. Some fancy stitching was done and I was sewn up again. I gave my surgeon a busy day.

When I came around the second time I looked at my friend in the next bed whose operation was to be after mine and got a great shock because she was up and walking around. My befuddled mind could not conceive how she had recovered enough from her hysterectomy to be walking about when I felt fit to die. Then she told me she was going home as her operation had to be cancelled because I had to go back the second time. I felt so sorry about that but was relieved that was the reason she was up and walking

Before surgery Robin and I decided that I would stay in hospital for the full 10 days to get a good rest and time to recover because as a telephone volunteer for the Miscarriage Association my days were often spent talking to people. That was the plan but again, it never happened. By day four, I was up and about, recovering well from the double hysterectomy. Walking slowly, but walking nonetheless. The pain was easing and I knew I would survive. I was starting to read and understood what I was reading. I was enjoying having my meals brought to me and having no dishes to wash. I loved having visitors and eating the chocolate they kindly gave me. Then came day five.

My husband came to visit me on day five and he looked terrible. In fact, he looked like he should have been in the bed instead of me. When I asked him what had happened, I couldn't believe his answer. That day in work he had lifted a heavy machine and felt something happen in his back. He got a shooting pain down his leg and had been in agony all day. When he asked if I could get home the next day, I thought that he was joking. He wasn't. I got permission to leave on the condition that I lifted nothing heavier than a teacup.

I came home and went to bed while Robin struggled to look after me. He was in terrible pain. Within a few days he was in the other bedroom and my next door neighbour came in and looked after both of us. As I started to recover, I became a carer. I drove Robin to hospitals, physio and doctors' appointments. After a year things got worse instead of better. Without any warning he began to fall. This was not only dangerous but made his injuries worse each time he went down. One particular fall left him trapped in a room with his head jammed against a door. It was a long time before he could move to let me in to see to him. Unfortunately that fall caused more damage, this time to his neck.

Robin's injuries have left him with permanent damage to his back and neck. Most days are a battle with pain and trying various methods to relieve it. He has never been able to return to work as he still has to spend a lot of time in bed. He attends the pain clinic and has been given great help there. This alternative lifestyle is not the one that we had in mind all those years ago but this is the one that God in His good providence had in mind for us, the one that He has chosen for us to live.

A day away for us may mean having a picnic in the garden. Making the most of summer days, I bring out the best china and we spend an hour watching the birds on the feeders as they watch us on the bench. We have had some lovely days. We are visited in the evenings and early mornings by foxes and badgers which we love to see. The scraps are kept for them and they have a little feeding area that they come to most evenings to see what they have got for supper. I have always called them Mrs Fox and Mr Badger. Obviously I don't know if they are Mr or Mrs, those are just my names for them. This gave us cause for laughter because one evening when we had guests for a meal I said,

"Don't worry if you can't eat it all, Mrs Fox will be up later to take it to her wee family."

Our guests thought Mrs Fox was one of our unfortunate neighbours who had fallen on bad times. When they realized I was talking about our furry friends, they doubled up laughing!

We had to devise a way to stop the roaming cats from stealing the food left for our visiting wildlife so Robin came up with the idea of putting a bin lid over the food and a brick on top. I thought they would never be able to lift it but they are

Badgers arrive for their supper.

amazing. The badgers just push their heads under the lid and eat with lid on their heads like a big hat. The foxes lift the lid by the handle and pull it away - all except one little fellow who was quite slow at catching on to the trick. He stood on the lid and walked around and around on it not knowing how to get at his supper. He looked very young.

So, while the world is sleeping, about 2.00am and 5.00am when Robin needs to get up because staying in bed is too painful, we get to see a lot of things that we would miss if we did not have this alternative lifestyle. This is the good side of how our lives are lived. There are other days that are not easy. We are very limited in what we can do. Some days take their toll. Hours of isolation and a sense of responsibility can leave me sad and vulnerable. These are the days when I literally run to God's Word. I lift His book and it comforts me like nothing else can. I read His Words,

"So do not fear, for I am with you, do not be dismayed, for I am your God. I will strengthen you and help you, I will uphold you with my righteous right hand." Isaiah 41. 10.

Like ointment applied to a wound, those words penetrate my sore heart. God will help me, it will be alright.

Chapter 44 ❧

CONTENTMENT

Contentment is not so much to do with our circumstances as our attitude towards our circumstances. That's why Paul could say, "Actually I don't have a sense of needing anything personally, I've learned by now to be quite content whatever my circumstances. I'm just as happy with little as much, with much as with little. I've found the recipe for being happy whether full or hungry, hands full or hands empty. Whatever I have, whatever I am, I can make it through anything in the One who makes me who I am." Philippians 4 v 10-14 (T.M.)

This recipe for happiness that Paul was talking about was not found in the easy life he had. No, just the opposite. This was a man who was beaten, tortured, imprisoned and starved. A man who did not always have enough money to get by, so he took on work. This was a man who knew about betrayal because even his friends deserted him at times. He tells us that at one of his court appearances, no-one came with him. Yet this was a man who made the right choices. He chose to trust God. He chose to praise God and he chose to have the right attitude in his circumstances. Because of these choices he was able to say that he was content.

Our attitude to the things that life throws at us will determine our peace. In his book "Blessed be Your Name", Matt Redman says,

"Contentment and trust build us up. Bitterness and complaint eat us up."

Walking by faith and not by sight is not always easy. It's hard to trust when things don't seem to be getting any better, maybe even getting worse. Our alternative lifestyle is a constant reminder of that struggle, but also a testimony to God's sufficiency. Bringing it down to practical everyday living is hard work.

Robin displays a wonderful attitude towards his suffering. Even on his worst days, he does not complain. Because of his neck problem, holding and reading a book is now too difficult. So he uses the computer to read the Bible and books that are spiritually uplifting. When people ask how he is, he says,

"I'm grand" or "I'm just fine."

When they ask me how he is I usually say,

"He's not great."

Robin says it depends on what way you look at it. To him he is fine because he trusts God totally for where he is at. He knows God has the power to heal him anytime but if He does not heal him, he knows God has him the way he is for a purpose and he is content. He could be bitter because the quality of his life has changed a lot. There are days when he can't stay out of bed for more than a few hours. He battles through dark days that come with no warning. On these days his motivation is low and he just wishes for tomorrow, in the hope that the dark cloud will have gone and he will feel better. But still, underneath it all, there is a peace that passes understanding, a contentment that not only builds him up but helps me focus on my own journey to contentment.

This personal journey has twists and turns, ups and downs, laughter and tears. I am learning to be adaptable for no two days are the same in our lives. I don't plan too far ahead because we have had to change too many plans. I am learning

Two Robins, easy going contented men.

many lessons on the journey. Mostly I am learning how important it is to have the right attitude. The road to contentment will not be found if I continually complain about my circumstances, or let self pity cloud my perspective. Brother Lawrence said, "We don't truly know peace in our hearts until pain is as welcome to us as the lack of it."

How do we get to that place? For me, I remind myself that God is walking this road with me. Not only does He know what I feel but He is allowing it. I may not understand all that is happening, but that's what faith is. Even if I never see the purpose behind what's happening, I choose to believe that God has a purpose. Often it is when we look back, we realize that God had a greater purpose for the things that brought us pain. When I think this way, my attitude changes. My heart finds peace. It is a surrender of my will, coming to that place where I can say and mean,

"Not my will but yours Lord."

It's found in my relationship with Him. John 14 v 4 says,

"Remain in me, and I will remain in you."

As I draw close to God, He comes and ministers His special grace and I am strengthened and built up once again. I cannot do it on my own. I am learning that only God can fill the lonely spaces in my life. The One who knows me by name is the Giver of Peace. The following poem expresses it so well.

The Solitary Way
By Charles E. Orr, from 'Food for Thought' 1904

There is a mystery in human hearts,
And though we be encircled by a host
Of those who love us well and are beloved.
To everyone of us from time to time,
There comes a sense of utter loneliness.
Our dearest friend is stranger to our joy
And cannot understand our bitterness and pain.
"There is not one to enter into all I feel"
Such is the cry of each of us in turn,
We wander in a "Solitary Way".
No matter what, or where our lot may be
Each heart mysterious to itself,
Must live its inner life in solitude.
And would you know the reason why this is?
It is because the Lord desires our love,
In every heart He wishes to be first.
He therefore keeps the secret key himself
To open all its chambers and to bless,
With perfect sympathy and holy peace
Each solitary soul that comes to Him.
So when we feel this loneliness, it is
The voice of Jesus saying "Come to me".
And every time we are "not understood."
It is a call to us to come again.
For Christ alone can satisfy the soul.
And those who walk with Him from day to day,
Can never have a "Solitary Way".

The journey continues.

Chapter 45

MONKEY ON A STICK

Do you remember the Rag man? You have to be a certain age to remember him.

The rag man came to our street once a week. His cart was pulled by a large brown horse that looked tired and sometimes a bit sad....... until he got a sweetie! I ran to the front of the cart to the horse while the other children ran to the back to see what the rag man was giving away in exchange for old clothes. Mostly he gave away plates and cups. Occasionally he had balloons.

This particular day though, I heard the other children squeal with delight as the rag man produced little toy monkeys that climbed up a wooden stick. We all ran to the house asking our mothers for rags for the rag man. My mother said she had none and chased me out. I was so disappointed because I really wanted a monkey on a stick. I ran in to the house again and tried pleading for rags and telling my mother about these toys again in case she had not taken it in the first time. She was losing patience with me by then and shouted at me to get out she had no rags. Then she finished by saying, "The only rags we have are the ones that's on us."

I left the house with the tears in my eyes at the thought that I would not get one of those monkeys on a stick. Then I thought of what my mother had said and I took off my good cardigan and I gave it to the rag man. I got my monkey on a stick and he got the only cardigan I owned.

I was about seven years old then and I knew that I had done something wrong. I took the monkey on a stick home and I hid it under my bed. That night when my mother asked me where my cardigan was, I said that I did not know.

I now had a monkey on a stick that I could not play with and I was cold because I had no cardigan. I had also told my mother a lie. I knew when she had found out what I had done I would get a smack. I was in trouble. The monkey on a stick was fast losing its appeal, after a while I did not even like looking at it.

A few days later my mother found it under my bed. I told her what I had done and she did give me a smack and, worse than the smack, kept reminding me of what a bad girl I had been. She didn't have the money to get me a new cardigan and that was what annoyed her the most. Eventually things settled down again. She was my mother, she loved me. She forgave me. I told her I would never give any more of my clothes to the rag man. I never did. I had learned my lesson.

Monkeys on sticks come in many disguises. We trade things that we shouldn't in order to get them only to realize that the price was too high and the trade wasn't worth it. Sometimes it's the same old monkey that we have to resist over and over again. Esau traded his birthright for a pot of stew. David traded his integrity for a woman called Bathsheba. Eve just had to have that fruit from the tree and we have all lived with the consequences ever since.

Only Christ can fill the empty spaces in our lives. He is enough. He is the all sufficient One. Only Christ can meet our deepest needs and our hearts are not satisfied until we realize that He is all we need. We are on a journey, one that will lead us to our heavenly home, He is our provision . These words from a worship song by Brian Doerksen say it all.

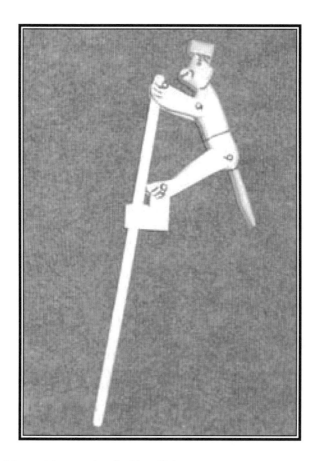

My soul is yearning for Your living stream,
My heart is aching for You
All that I long for is found in Your heart,
You are everything I need.

You are the thirst,
You are the stream
You are the hunger living deep inside of me,
You are the food that satisfies,
You are provision for the journey of our lives,
You are everything,
You are.

Have you ever felt that hunger deep inside? The ache for God Himself to come and satisfy the longing in your heart. Sometimes there are vacuums in our lives. If we don't fill them with God it is all too easy to fill them with other things. We do it to feel better but often end up feeling worse.

The following story is an example of what I mean.

Paul our youngest boy never liked school, he just did not feel comfortable there and was always looking for an excuse to stay at home. Sore head, sore throat, sore ears and sore stomach were the usual complaints. I soon learned to be prepared for these early morning ailments and had a supply of most of the medicines required to bring about a cure for anything, real or imagined.

One morning Paul complained about sore ears.

"Don't worry, Mammy will get the ear drops and it will soon be better." I said.

"Do you not think that I need to stay home from school?" Paul asked.

"No Paul, these drops will make everything better in a day or two." I replied.

I put the drops in his ears for the next four days and by that time there should have been an improvement. The ears were still hurting Paul said. I thought that I would check the bottle in case they were out of date. What I saw on the bottle gave me such a shock. 'For Veterinary use only', it said. I had been putting rabbit drops in Paul's ears. I was horrified.

I phoned my friend who is a doctor and told him the story. He laughed and asked me, "Have his ears grown any?"

I felt so sorry for Paul - no wonder he was still complaining with sore ears! The drops that I gave him would never have worked because Paul was a boy, not a rabbit. In trying to make him better, I made him worse. I did it because the outside of the bottle looked like the outside of the bottle I needed. However, the stuff inside the bottle was not what I thought it was and that's what made the difference.

Some of the things that I have used over the years to fill some empty spaces in my life looked alright. After a while though, I realized that they did not do what I thought they would. Sometimes they made the situation worse. They did not take the pain away. They certainly did not make things better.

Our comfort, peace and identity are found in Christ alone. He speaks into our lives as He did to the woman at the well. He offers us living water and says,

"Whoever drinks the water that I give him will never thirst. Indeed, the water I give him will become in him a spring of water welling up to eternal life." John 4 v14.

So I come like this woman before me and say,

"Give me this water."

He is our source. He is our peace. The empty places in our lives can only be filled with Him, God alone. He does what He says He will do. As we draw close to Him our strength is renewed like the eagle's and our hungry hearts are satisfied.

Chapter 46 ❧

ANSWERED PRAYER

Have you ever had prayers that were answered, but not in the way that you thought they would be? Have you had prayers that were never answered at all?

Maybe you have had to wait a long time for the answer and you have wondered why it had to take so long. Why is Gods' time scale so different to ours? I think it is because God wants to do more than answer our prayers, He has a greater purpose than we know and as we wait He works in our lives to change us into the people that He wants us to be. The waiting is not easy and at times we feel like giving up, we become desperate. I have known those times and as I thought about women of the Bible who prayed prayers that came from brokenness and pain, I tried for just a little while, to put myself in their place. Having lost children of my own, Hannah was the one that I could identify with the most. After reading Hannah's story one day as I sat in silence, the following thoughts made their way on to paper.

When you're desperate you pray. When you're desperate you make promises, you vow vows that don't seem hard to carry out because nothing could be worse than your present pain. Hannah was desperate that day she came to the temple to pray. Her heart hurt so much it felt like it had blisters on it. That was the day she prayed, that was the day she made the vow.

"Lord if you give me a son I will give him to you all the days of his life."

And so he was born, Samuel, a beautiful dark haired, dark eyed boy.

When Hannah looked at him lying there in her arms her blistered heart started to heal.

Samuel - he just had to smile and her world changed. How would she ever let him go? Why did she make that promise? But she had. She had made a vow to the Holy One and she could not go back on her word.

The day came when she had to keep her promise. Hannah found an old sack and started to fill it with Samuel's things. His little coat that she had made for him. The rope that Elkanah had cut to tie around his waist holding his tunic in place. Then, lying in the corner, she saw the little cart that Elkanah had patiently carved for his son to play with. Samuel loved that cart. She was tempted to keep it - she needed a reminder of her little boy's presence, but he needed it more. As she put it in the sack, the tears flowed down her face. This would be the last night that Samuel would sleep in this house. How would they live without him?

That night as she tucked Samuel up in his little bed she thought that her heart would break. He was three years old. It was time.

"Why are you crying Mummy?" Samuel asked.

"Mummy's not crying," she said as she tried to wipe the tears away. "You have to go to sleep early tonight, we have a long journey tomorrow."

"Where are we going?" he asked.

"We are going to the temple, Samuel, to learn how to pray."

"Why have you packed a sack Mummy?"

How could she tell him? What could she tell him?

She reached down and took her son in her arms and as he put his chubby little arms around her neck, Hannah told Samuel where they were going. She told him he was a special boy and how God had a plan for his life. She watched while he fell asleep. Tonight she did not want to sleep, she would always remember him as he was tonight, this night. The look on his sleeping face would have to last a lifetime.

The morning came too quickly. They got up and prepared for the journey. As they approached the temple they saw old Eli standing there. Would he be kind to Samuel? Would he come to him if he cried in the night? Hannah had to trust the Holy One as never before.

She kissed Samuel and gave him to Eli and said,"This is the child that I prayed for and now I give him to the Lord for his whole life."

Hannah had prayed for a child for a long time.

God answered her prayer in His time ......and probably in a way that she could never have dreamed possible. Part of that waiting was to bring Hannah to a different place in her relationship with God and enable her to be part of a much bigger plan.

W.E.Binderwolf said, "If Hannah's prayers for a son had been answered at the time she had set for herself, the nation might not have known the mighty man of God it found in Samuel. Hannah wanted only a son, but God wanted more. He wanted a prophet, a saviour and a ruler for his people. Someone said 'God had to get a woman before he could get a man'. This woman he got in Hannah. Precisely by those weeks, months, and years there came a woman with a vision like God's with tempered soul and gentle spirit and a well seasoned will, prepared to be the kind of a woman for the kind of a man God knew the nation needed."

More and more I am coming to understand that God has a bigger picture than I know about, that if God does not answer my prayers when I think He should, there is a good reason.

Looking back at some of the prayers that God did not answer, I can see that there was a bigger plan and through that different plan, something changed in me. This has not always been easy, because it is not easy to let go of our dreams. However, this wonderful, merciful Saviour who sees the end from the beginning, calls us to trust Him, nurturing Hannah hearts that will love Him enough to believe He will bring us through even when we have to give Him back our dreams. The story of Hannah is a wonderful story of answered prayer. It is also a story of obedience and surrender.

Chapter 47 🕊

AUTUMN

I don't know how I got to be this old so soon. I call myself middle aged but that is now stretching it a bit. I don't know any 116 year olds! I suppose these are the Autumn years of life. Spring and Summer certainly passed very quickly. Autumn is well on its way and perhaps I will be here for Winter. I find that I am slowing down physically and making changes in my lifestyle.

My work with The Miscarriage Association finished this summer after 18 years. I gave my last lecture in Queen's University. I had stopped taking the help line calls 2 years ago and now a group of women carry the work forward. Claire worked with me almost from the beginning and others have come along over the years wanting to help because they received help. I still have contact with most of them. Two have retyped this book for me and another one encouraged me to write it.

Over the years as I have met with my prayer partners, we have prayed for many of them. I always referred to them affectionately as "my lambs". I am so proud of them and what they have achieved and what they have brought to the organization. They now have lambs of their own and care for them in various ways as they lead them through the pain that the loss of a baby brings. They are all well qualified to do it. I have stood with them as they buried their sons and daughters. They have known the loss of hope and watched their dreams die as they picked coffins instead of prams. I have worked for months with others who did not have a baby to bury and helped them find ways to make memories for a little life that ended before it was born. Some are still waiting for their miracle, I wait prayerfully with them. I have gone through subsequent pregnancies with so many that for 16 years I felt as if I was continually pregnant myself. I was ready for a rest and yet, I would say that they often gave me more than I gave them.

I have had the privilege of being part of a very special group of women who have faced loss with courage. I can honestly say that I never found it a burden. I loved and prayed for each one knowing that there was One who loved them much more than I ever could. I am thankful that out of my own pain God opened this door. It is very hard to see any good in the loss of a baby. For me the one good thing was taking the pain and walking with others through theirs. Encouraging them that they would make it through even though there was a void in their lives that the whole world could not fill. Ralph Waldo Emerson said, "It is one of the most beautiful compensations in life, we can never help another without being helped ourselves."

How very true that statement is. My years with The Miscarriage Association have changed me. I have become Mother, Sister and Friend. Mostly I was an ear to listen, or a pair of arms to hug. The organization was at a pioneering stage when I took the role as figurehead. It was great to be part of those formative years and I'd like to think that I made a difference. Certainly I have seen positive changes over the years in how women are cared for when they have lost a baby. I did not do it alone of course, we all played our parts as we were gifted. Claire has represented us at hundreds of committee meetings which would have killed me. It is a good thing to know what your gifts are and let others use theirs who are more able. I enjoyed teaching at study days and working with the medical profession. We learnt from each other and we have all come a long way since those early days.

Now the time has come to move on. I want to concentrate more on speaking. I would also love to host Victorian Tea parties. Small groups where women can come and rest for a few hours enjoying time out and a chat over a cup of tea. So much of our lives are taken up with busyness. When we bring out the teapot and the fine china we create an atmosphere of a different era, when life was not so hurried and taking tea was a treat. I hope that as we share our tea we will share ourselves too. I would like it to be a place of refreshment from which people will leave more able to face the challenges of modern living and all that entails.

New chapters in our lives are not only exciting, they are scary too. Yet this God calls those of us who serve Him to be people of pilgrimage, in other words people who move on. It is easier to do what we have always done. Moving out of our comfort zone always involves risk. Psalm 84 v 5&6 says,

Lavinia hosting a Victorian tea party for her prayer partners, Gloria, Pat and Gwen.

"Blessed are those whose strength is in You who have set their hearts on pilgrimage. As they pass through the Valley of Baca they make it a place of Springs, the Autumn rains also cover it with pools. They go from strength to strength till each one appears before Zion."

I want my life in these Autumn years to leave those refreshing pools wherever I go. Maybe even bring them into Winter. Then......... the other side of the door. C.S.Lewis in one of his books, "The Weight of Glory" says, "At present we are on the outside of the world, the wrong side of the door. We discern the purity and freshness of the morning but they do not make us fresh and pure. We cannot mingle with the splendours we see. But all the leaves of the New Testament are rustling with the rumour that it will not always be so. Someday God willing we shall get in."

I have felt the pull of that day for many years now. That day will just be the beginning. The beginning of something that will never end. What a day that will be - the Bible often refers to it as "that day". My heart has been drawn towards heaven for many years, in fact for as long as I can remember, there has always been a part of me that is homesick for another land. My eternal home. As good as it gets here I know deep inside that there is a place waiting for me that is indescribable. A place of joy and peace. A place where not another tear will be shed. Where there will be no more goodbyes. All the secrets of heaven are not revealed to us so I will not try to describe the indescribable. I do know this - we shall see the King, Jesus. He will be the focus of our worship and adoration and as we gaze on Him our hungry hearts will be satisfied.

As a young woman in deep despair after the loss of one of my babies I said to my Pastor, "Someday the Lord will tell me why."

He was a very wise man. He could have agreed, trying to make it easier for me. Instead he said, "I think when we see Christ in all His beauty and the joys of heaven we will say, 'There was something I was going to ask You, but I forget what it was now.'"

Pastor Forsythe was always encouraging us to keep our eyes on another land. Heaven.

Although my heart has run on ahead of me to that place and "that day", I have some time yet here. I may long for heaven but that will not take away from the joy that life still brings now. There is a little bit more to do. I am between two worlds. Until then my heart will go on singing. He will lead and guide me into the future as He always has. My tomorrows are in His hands.

But........that's another tale.

Epilogue ᔕ

LEAVES IN AUTUMN

"Let Me show you one of My favourite scenes in the kingdom," said the Master with such anticipation in His voice that I left what I had been doing and followed eagerly in His footsteps. It was Autumn once more and as we walked, the fallen leaves crunched beneath our feet.

We followed the trail into a forested area and soon I was surrounded on every side by tall, majestic trees. The distinctive scent of pine pervaded the air and sounds from beyond the forest were silenced by the density of the trees. I glanced at the Master, wondering in my heart if these magnificent trees were what He had been so enthusiastic about – trees that stayed tall and green all year round.

He smiled and, as usual, read my mind.

"No, we still have some way to go," He answered my unspoken question.

Some time later, we reached a clearing in the forest, a huge, roughly circular grassy area. I walked into the centre of this arena and sat down on a moss-covered tree stump. As I breathed in the perfume of grass and trees, I closed my eyes and felt my shoulders fall and my whole body relax. What a wonderful place – a green space protected by the tall green trees of the forest – quiet and so peaceful.

"This is like a great, natural cathedral," I thought. "I could worship the King here. Surely this is what He wanted to show me."

When I opened by eyes, the Master was smiling but also shaking His head.

"You're right in one respect," He told me. "This is a place where you might encounter the King and it would indeed be easy to worship Him here in the stillness. But it's not where I'm leading you today."

I rose from the tree stump and somewhat reluctantly followed the Master out of the clearing and back into the comparative darkness of the forest. The path twisted and turned as it snaked up the hillside and I kept stumbling over tree roots that had broken through the surface. It wasn't long before I was feeling tired and I longed to be back in the clearing.

"I'm not as young as I used to be," I grumbled to the Master. "It's all very well for the young ones to be taken trekking high in the forest but I don't have the energy for a steep climb like this."

He moved closer to my side and drew my arm through His.

"Let's do it together," He encouraged. "It's not much further and it will be worth it in the end."

Within a few moments, we had crested a ridge and there spread out before us was a long valley filled almost entirely by a lake. As we walked down the hill, a gentler slope on this side of the ridge, I became aware that we were no longer surrounded by evergreen trees but by deciduous trees, whose leaves were responding to the call of Autumn by changing colour.

The Master found a fallen log near the water's edge and we sat down together.

"This is what I wanted to show you" He said softly, "the glory of the trees in Autumn. Sit for a moment and savour the beauty."

What a sight met my eyes. The leaves of the tree under which I sat were like burnished bronze, while the one next to it was covered in deep orange, almost red leaves. Nearby, the bright yellow leaves of a chestnut tree waved gently in the breeze, while yet another tree beside it was dressed in foliage of bright pink. The entire lake was encircled in similar displays of such beauty that they took my breath away. The dazzling scene was reflected in the still water of the lake, redoubling the effect and where the sun shone, the colours glowed even brighter.

It was one of those moments in Kingdom Park that I wanted to hold on to, the memory of which would bring solace when I had to face a dark day. Then the Master began to speak and His words burned deep into my soul.

"You said on the way here that you're not as young as you used to be – well that is partly why I wanted you to see the splendour of this scene and learn the lesson of the leaves in Autumn. These leaves have been hard at work since Spring – taking in sunlight and rain and playing a vital role in helping the tree to grow. Now they are changing colour and it may seem that their work is over."

"Oh yes," I interrupted, "that's just how I feel sometimes and I know my friends feel like that too now and again. We have worked hard in Kingdom Park but we don't have the energy to do what we used to do. Sometimes it feels as though we have lost our value, that we're a bit useless now."

"Tell Me," asked the Master with a twinkle in His eye, "how did the Autumn leaves make you feel when I showed them to you?"

"They made my heart sing with delight – they were so beautiful," I replied.

"Well, Child," the Master informed me, "that's how the King feels when He looks at you in this Autumn season. You may not have the strength to work as hard for the Kingdom but you can be beautiful, more beautiful than at any other time in your life. And it gives great pleasure to the King when He sees you putting on a dazzling display for His glory."

I did feel better for a moment or two as I gazed once more at the glowing colours but then a sadness rose from deep within me. Those beautiful leaves would soon die and fall from the trees and they reminded me of my own mortality. The Master sensed my change of mood and moved closer to reassure me.

"It's not the end for the leaves when thy die, you know," He whispered. "When they fall and decay, they create nourishing food for the future life of the tree, food for future leaves and food for future fruit. In a similar way, the things you say and do will live on after you, providing nourishing food to help future generations to live and grow and produce fruit – like a rich spiritual compost!"

I laughed at the thought of being compost and the Master laughed with me, then He added, "Autumn does lead to the dark, cold days of Winter. It can be a time of loss and emptiness and harsh circumstances but don't fear it. I'll be just as close to you in Winter as in the bright, sunny days of Summer – maybe even a little closer! Every Winter holds the promise of Spring, the promise of rebirth, renewal and new life."

A great smile lit up His face, a smile that spoke of secret knowledge and deep mysteries.

"You have no idea what the Spring will be like – such wonder, such riches......everything made new......being able to look on the face of the King......So don't fear the Winter that leads you there."

"And Child," He went on, His voice resonating with joy and delight. "Some leaves get the chance to fly before they fall – carried along by the wind, twirling and turning in an exciting dance, soaring high into the sky. Some of them manage to fly a long way and even create compost for other trees in the forest."

I caught some of His enthusiasm and my heart beat faster. Maybe Autumn in Kingdom Park would turn out to be the most exciting season of them all! Maybe I too could put on a spectacular display for the King, glowing with the brightest colours, bringing glory to His Name and pleasure to His heart. And maybe, just maybe, I would get to fly as I yielded my life to the wind of His Spirit, soaring and dancing as He carried me through Winter into His eternal Spring.

Gloria Kearney

❧

You can contact LAVINIA *by email at*
laviniaabrol@gmail.com
www.ambassador-productions.com

❧